D1120768

THE TAKEOVER

Everything You Need To Know About Business

BY

LA'FOY ORLANDO THOMAS III

King of Urban Education

Visit "www.BlackBusinessSmart.blogspot.com"

Bloomington, IN Milton Keynes, UK

authorHOUSE

AuthorHouse™
1663 Liberty Drive, Suite 200
Bloomington, IN 47403
www.authorhouse.com
Phone: 1-800-839-8640

AuthorHouse™ UK Ltd.
500 Avebury Boulevard
Central Milton Keynes, MK9 2BE
www.authorhouse.co.uk
Phone: 08001974150

© 2006 La'Foy Orlando Thomas III. All rights reserved.

No part of this book may be reproduced, stored in a retrieval system, or transmitted by any means without the written permission of the author.

First published by AuthorHouse 10/17/2006

ISBN: 1-4259-6221-1 (sc)

Library of Congress Control Number: 2006909013

Printed in the United States of America
Bloomington, Indiana

This book is printed on acid-free paper.

CONTENTS

ACKNOWLEDGEMENTS

I first want to thank God the Father for his ever enduring mercy, and even more so for sending his son Jesus Christ to die for my sins. Second, I want to thank my Lord and Savior Jesus Christ for dying for my sins, and for being the perfect mediator between me and the Father every time I mess up. I know that you love me, and I ask that you help me to love you with my actions the way that you love me with yours. Without you, I or this book doesn't exist. Thank you!!!

Third, I want to thank my beautiful (inside & out) wife Camille, for all the love and support that you've given me. Thank you for allowing me to spend me entire weekends from 7am to 12 am midnight to complete this project. I love you!

Fourth, I want to thank all of my college instructors who played a monumental role in preparing me to write this book with the knowledge that was poured into me in class. Special thanks go to Mr. Dougherty, Mr. Dave Martin, and Jim Muck. Not only did you guys pour knowledge into me, but also instilled me with confidence as well. It meant more to me than you probably know. Thank you!

Fifth, I want to thank all the radio stations, BET, Oprah, The NAACP, National Black Chamber of Commerce-Harry C. Alford, Russell Simmons, Shawn Carter, Black Enterprise, Dr. Creflo Dollar, Bishop TD Jakes, Reverend William Owens, Bishop G.E. Patterson, Bishop Darrell Hines, Dr. Frederick K.C. Price, Bishop Eddie Long, Rainbow Push Coalition, Essence Magazine, Upscale Magazine, Jet Magazine, Ebony Magazine, Sister 2 Sister, XXL Magazine, Vibe Magazine, TV One, YWCA-Peggy Sanchez Mills, Shirley Franklin-Mayor of Atlanta, GA, Anthony Williams-Mayor of Washington, DC, and John F. Street-Mayor of Philadelphia, PA. I want to thank each and every one of you for helping to get this product in the hands of our people. Lord knows we are in need. I'm thanking all of you in advance because I'm praying to God in the name of Jesus that you all will play monumental roles in the success of this book, and I have faith that it will be done. So THANKYOU!!!

Last but not least, I want to thank my mother Veronica Hutchins-Jordan for carrying me for nine months, and for whooping me on the kitchen floor for sneaking off to watch wrestling, when I was supposed to be learning to spell Grass and Green. Yep, I still remember.

To my brother Brandon…I love you man! To my sister Breonna…I love you! My sister Janae….I love you. My sister Jasmine…..Be good! My sister Samone….Remind your big sister Jasmine to be good. I love you all!

Anyone I forgot, blame my head, and not my heart. I love you and God Bless!

PREFACE:

The world of investing can be a very scary place for many people, especially poor people who haven't been properly educated on the matter. Unfortunately many Americans have depended upon the school system including college to teach us and our children about the important lessons of business and finance.

The problem is that most public school systems, especially those that hold class for mainly poverty stricken students don't have curriculums on the subjects of business, finance, investing, and real estate on the high school level, unlike many suburban public schools that hold class for mainly students from well to do families.

For example, I went to a high school in Milwaukee, WI for three years (I graduated a year early) that was mainly a poor Black school. At the time, my high school didn't have any classes available on economics, accounting, marketing, real estate investing or any other business related classes that would have been fundamental to my financial preparing.

On the other hand, my wife went to a suburban public high school housed to mainly financially stable White students. To no surprise of mine, they had classes on economics, accounting, marketing, business, and many other important classes that continue to give "certain" students a head start, which is one of the many reasons, the poor continue to lag behind the rich in many vital areas including homeownership, median household income, and college graduates.

The good news is that everything that you need to know about money and investing that the school system didn't teach you will be given to you as you read this book. This book will give detailed information on the important subjects of business and investing including stocks, bonds, options trading, business plans, business entities, real estate investing, mortgages, accounting, contracts, marketing and economics. Each chapter is dedicated to one of the subjects at hand and will give you all the basics and some advanced knowledge that will fully prepare you to operate in that realm of business or investing.

After you read this book you will have as much business and investment knowledge as some MBA's have after $70,000 of business school training from some of the most prestigious schools in the world including Harvard, Yale, Stanford, Wharton, and Cornell to name a few.

The lessons that I will share with you in this book will give you all you need to become very wealthy and open up many doors of opportunity for those around you with the knowledge you will possess after reading the last page of this book. I ask that you help me help our people overcome their deficiencies in these important areas of business by using the best marketing there is: word of mouth and encourage everyone you know to buy this book and visit "www.BlackBusinessSmart.blogspot.com" and together lets close the gap! God Bless You!!!

CHAPTER 1
THE NEED FOR INVESTING

The need for education on business and investing has never been more crucial than it is today. Rather it be in real estate, stocks, or investing your life savings into a small business, positioning our money in an environment where it can grow is a necessity if we are going to catch up and level the playing field with our more fortunate counter parts that control the majority of wealth in this country.

The difference in investing philosophies between the rich and the poor can be compared to two farmers: both farmers are given corn and apple seeds, but due to the way they were raised, they decide to do two different things with their seeds.

The first farmer is wise and plants his seeds in good soil were he knows he will reap a very large harvest in the future that will allow him to continue to eat and re plant seeds on a continual basis for the rest of his life.

The second farmer wasn't raised with the same principles as the first farmer and instead of planting his seeds in good soil, he decides to hide some of his seeds under his mattress, while throwing the rest in the garbage. As time past, the seeds under his mattress aren't as valuable as they were before, and no longer can harvest all the fruit that they could have if planted originally. To make this scenario even worse, the first farmer was given twice as much seed as the second farmer, emphasizing the importance for the second farmer to be more careful with how he utilized his seeds.

This analogy is very similar to what happens today between the rich and the poor. The rich constantly spend their money on assets that will continually bring positive cash flow, thus allowing them to eat off the original seeds for a very long time.

On the other hand, the poor will often spend their hard earned money on junk or other futile possessions, that have little to no chance of an appreciated resale value, thus the equivalent to throwing them in the garbage.

The reason for this book is to influence everyone who has made it a way of life to get some money, spend it all on something that isn't worth anything, and then repeat the process, further perpetuating a life time of struggle.

The scariest part about this way of living is that small children are often the victim. Not only are they not given an opportunity to have financially stable childhoods, but they often are influenced by the behavior of their parents, and end up following the same hopeless procedures, and then of course passing this same dead end way of thinking down from generation to generation.

When a person is educated on the levels of business and finance, he or she can be comfortable making wise investment decisions that he or she did not know existed. For example: When I was 17 years old, I had no idea of what the stock market was. I didn't know what Wall Street was, and I definitely didn't know who Dow Jones was.

As time went on and I became educated on these subjects, I became very comfortable making my own investment decisions with stocks and mutual funds, and later on with real estate, which has become my favorite investment of all.

You may ask why real estate is my favorite investment of all, and the answer is quite simple: LEVERAGE! We will cover this subject in great detail in a later chapter, but basically what leverage does is give you a great opportunity to prosper off of OPM (other people's money).

To my knowledge, real estate is the only investment where you can borrow 100% of the money and have a third person (tenant) pay the bank back, while still owning 100% of the property. Once the asset appreciates in value and you sell, all of the profit belongs to you, and doesn't need to be shared with the bank who gave you 100% of the money, or with the tenants who politely paid your mortgage for you.

I can't stress how important it is to do something positive with your money before you decide to go blow it on futile possessions such as fancy cars, gaudy jewelry, and the latest $1200 Prada bag. It's not that you can't have these nice things because you can. I'm just saying don't spend your hard earned money to get them, but instead spend your hard earned money on an asset, like a nice piece of property that has a continual positive cash flow, that you can then spend however you please.

The key is to put your money in an environment where it can continue to grow and spit more seeds out, thus giving you a life time of harvest. On the other hand, if you get your money and buy all junk with it, the opportunity for harvest doesn't exist, and the seeds are practically thrown in the garbage. For more information on the need for investing, visit www.BlackBusinessSmart.blogspot.com.

CHAPTER 2
WHAT YOU NEED TO KNOW ABOUT ECONOMICS

How well a particular investment performs is generally influenced by the state of the economy. Before learning about a specific investment, I feel it is essential to learn about the economy and the impact it has on the world of investing. Also it is very important to know what economic cycle you are in, and therefore know how to adjust and react to each climate accordingly.

The economy is measured by several economic indicators that take the temperature of the economy, and some indicators even give a future forecast on what is expected of the economy in the future.

Of all the economic indicators, some are more important than others. The most important economic indicator is considered by many as the parent indicator, and that is the GDP or Gross Domestic Product. The GDP is the total dollar value of all goods and services produced by labor and property in the United States. A GDP that is increasing signifies an economic growth cycle that may cause inflation, were a GDP on the decline signifies an economy that is slowing down that has the potential to cause deflation.

The GDP report measures quarterly activity and has a heavy influence on how people invest and spend their money. The report is released three times each quarter, being revised each time to finally come up with a final report for the quarter during the last month of the next quarter. For example, the final revision of the GDP report for the first quarter (January-March) would be released in June, and can be found on the YAHOO! Finance page with all other indicators.

Keeping good track of the GDP growth (or decline) numbers should give you a good feel for the state of the economy and also let you know what phase of the business or economic cycle you are currently in. There are generally five phases in the business cycle as outlined below:

Business/Economic Cycle

1.) **Downturn:** Starting from the peak (highpoint) in the economy, the downturn starts when the GDP has its' first quarter of negative growth, and last for as long as the GDP report is signifying negative growth. Two consecutive quarters of negative GDP growth is officially considered a recession. During a downturn, investors generally get nervous and begin to dump quality investments for less than market value. At this time, investment bargains are usually easy to come by.

2.) **Trough:** The trough signifies the end of the downturn or recession. It represents the lowest level in the business cycle. During a trough, because it is the lowest phase in the cycle, reports start to improve and the economy is getting ready to bounce back. In my opinion this is the best time to invest, especially in real estate and stocks. Due to a lack of consumer confidence at this point in the cycle, investments are usually at their lowest point. Once you're at the bottom, the only way you can go is up, so I advise you buy all the quality real estate and stocks as possible.

3.) **Recovery:** The recovery begins when the GDP growth is positive again. The recovery is over when the GDP level surpasses the previous peak in the previous business cycle, thus is the start of an expansion.

4.) **Expansion:** An expansion occurs when the GDP rate is reaching new heights, and last until it reaches a new peak. At this point, investments normally are costing more than they are really worth. During this phase of the cycle, be careful in what you buy, because the peak is coming and on its way. If you buy too close to the top, you'll have to sale on the way back down, thus taking a loss.

5.)   Peak: The peak is the highest point in the business cycle. In my opinion this is the worst time to start investing because once you're at the top, the only way you can go is down.

Now that we have a good understanding of the economic cycle, we can now go in depth on all of my other favorite economic reports/indicators that generally give you a clue in what direction the economy is headed before the GDP report is even released.

Although there are many economic indicators viewed and adhered to by Wall Street, there are only six of them besides the GDP report that I find important as they are listed below:

Important Economic Indicators

1.)   Consumer Price Index (CPI): The CPI measures the level of inflation or increase in prices for goods and services in the marketplace. Inflation is generally high during times of expansion and lower during a downturn. During an expansion, people are spending money at new levels and the high demand for goods and services generally allows businesses to raise there prices. Generally, when inflation is growing too rapidly, the Federal Reserve will take action to raise interest rates, which will make money not as easy to borrow, and slow down the crazy shopping, that in return slows down the inflation. The CPI report is released monthly, approximately two weeks after the month ends.

2.)   Employment Report: The employment report contains information such as the unemployment rate, payrolls, and hourly wages. This report is very important as it is one of the first indicators each month of what direction the economy is going in. In times of an expansion or growing economy, payrolls are usually up, and the unemployment rate is usually down and vice versa for times of a downturn or a recession. This report is also released monthly on the first Friday of every month.

3.) **Retail Sales:** The retail sales report is one of my favorite reports, as it gives us the level of consumer spending, which accounts for approximately 2/3rds of the Gross Domestic Product. Generally when retail sales are up, inflation shortly follows as it shows an increased demand in consumer goods. This report is usually released in the middle of every month.

4.) **Consumer Confidence:** The consumer confidence index gives a reflection of how consumers feel about the current and future state of the economy or business cycle. A decrease in consumer confidence usually causes a decrease in retail sales, thus causing a decrease in the GDP. When consumers are not comfortable about the current or future state of the economy, they usually tighten their belts and decrease their level of spending due to worries that hard times may be coming ahead. During an expansion (good times), consumer confidence is generally high as the job market is generally good and most of their investments may have reached new highs. The consumer confidence report usually comes out the last week of every month.

5.) **Housing Starts:** Along with the retail sales report, the housing starts report is one of my favorite reports. The housing starts report details the number of single and multifamily homes being built. As we all know, when a home is built and then purchased, it calls for further spending on appliances, fixtures, and other household related goods. This report gives us a pretty solid indication of where the economy is going approximately 3-6 months ahead of time. The housing starts report is released monthly and is heavily watched by Wall Street.

6.) **Durable Goods:** Durable goods can be described as goods with a life expectancy of at least two to three years. Durable goods would include such items as washers, dryers, stoves, computers, and other long lasting items bought by consumers and businesses alike. Durable goods sales are generally up in an expanding economy and down in times of downturn and recession. This report is also released monthly, approximately three weeks after the reporting month ends.

Supply & Demand

One of the most important, yet simple aspects of economics is supply and demand. Generally, when the supply of something is high and the demand for it is low, then the price for that item generally declines. When the supply of something is low and the demand for it is high, then prices generally increase since there are more buyers than product available.

This aspect is very clear in today's society, as when the demand for gas or housing goes up, the price usually goes up with it, especially if the demand is much higher than the supply.

On the other hand, if the demand for something is low say at Wal-Mart or Target, and the supply of that item is high, the item usually goes on clearance to entice shoppers to buy, when they would otherwise not even bother.

This also is the case when department stores have clearance sales to get rid of old trends or fashions that are no longer demanding the attention of consumers. An example of this would be in the winter season and summer clothes are marked down to their lowest points. This is because the demand for summer clothes is very low in the winter time, thus needing an extremely low price to entice consumers.

Another scenario is when the demand and supply of something is approximately equal. This is considered the equilibrium point, and prices generally stay the same except for some minor adjustments due to inflation.

Having your finger on the pulse of the economy is critical if you are going to have long term success with investing or if you plan on having a successful business operation.

Generally in times of a bad market or downturn, most businesses decrease their spending and tighten their belts as much as possible. As stated by Robert Kiyosaki, during times of a bad market, I think that extra spending should be done on advertising and other marketing to give your business or product as much exposure as possible.

During hard times, the more you cut your cost that bring in business for you/generate sales, the more your business is going to suffer and sales are going to decrease.

As with investing, it is unwise to buy real estate or stocks at inflated prices during the high points of an expansion or peak in the economy, but without the proper education, one can't possible know what is considered a good or bad time in the economy.

On the other hand, I recommend buying under priced real estate and stocks during bad times and hold until the market recovers. During the hard times in the economy, people are often scared and make decisions based on that emotion, and sell very good investments for much less than they are worth.

Likewise, when the economy is strong, people are more than willing to buy over inflated investments, because they always think it can only get better, forgetting the last recession that took place only a few years earlier.

I believe it was Warren Buffet who said it best, "be greedy when others are fearful, and fearful when others are greedy".

Summary of Chapter

When investing, knowing your economic conditions is just as, if not more important than a diabetic knowing their blood sugar level. It is critical, as not knowing this vital information could put you in a position to loose all of your money and then cause you to miss out on possible riches in the future, as you will probably blame the particular investment for your loss, instead the real culprit: YOU! For more information on economics, visit the world popular www.BlackBusinessSmart.blogspot.com.

CHAPTER 3
WHAT YOU NEED TO KNOW ABOUT REAL ESTATE INVESTING

In the world of investing, there are practically hundreds, if not thousands of different investment options for an investor to choose from. Often, many people are advised that the best investment choices are in various stocks or mutual funds.

Generally, when you question someone who makes this ignorant statement they will tell you how stocks have grown over 10% over the last 75 years and so on and so forth. I consider this an ignorant statement because it's an ignorant statement.

In many cases, investing in stocks can be a good decision to help add diversity to your portfolio, but in no way should it be the main piece of your investment puzzle. The reason why stocks shouldn't be your main thing in your portfolio is the huge benefit you get from investing in real estate.

To my knowledge, there are no banks that will borrow you $1,000,000 to purchase $1,000,000 worth of stocks. This is for several reasons, but the biggest reason is that stocks can be very risky, and a bad stock portfolio can go from being valued at $1,000,000 to less than $1,000 in the matter of a few weeks, such as the case with Enron and World Com stock.

On the other hand, if your credit score is good, there are thousands of mortgage lenders that will give you 100% financing for a property worth that same $1,000,000 that they wouldn't dare borrow you to invest in stocks.

Now let's do some math: If you invest $100,000 out of your own pocket in stocks and the stock market has a good year and your portfolio raises by 20%, your portfolio would then be worth $120,000 on a $20,000 or 20% gain.

To some people this is great. A dream come true to a novice investor. They made $20,000 in one year just by having their money in a few good stocks, or at least a few stocks that had a good year. What more could an investor ask for, one might ask? The answer to that question is a whole lot more.

Let's use a similar scenario in the world of real estate. Although in many cases a mortgage lender will borrow you 100% of the purchase price of a property, my next scenario will involve a real estate investor having a 10% down payment on a million dollar property.

In this case, the investor puts as a down payment $100,000 of their own money into a $1,000,000 piece of real estate. Let's assume that the real estate market had a good year, but not quite as good as the stock market. Remember, in the stock market scenario we assumed a 20% increase in the portfolio, but we are only going to assume a 10% increase in the real estate investor's property for that same year.

Looking at raw numbers, you may think that stocks were the best option during the year under review, but then we take a closer look.

With the $1,000,000 piece of real estate, a 10% increase is a gain of $100,000, which is equivalent to the total investment made by the investor, giving them a 100% profit in only a one year period.

In the two above scenarios we had two investments of $100,000 each, but because of the power of leverage, the real estate investment of $100,000 was able to get the investor a $1,000,000 investment. So even when we assumed the stock market had a much better year then the real estate market, it shows that it's still in your best interest to have real estate as the largest piece of your investment puzzle.

Another reason why stocks are riskier than real estate is because real estate is what we consider "real property". Property can be divided between real property and personal property.

Real property is land and anything permanently attached to it, such as trees, buildings and anything permanently attached to the building. Personal property would be anything else, such as clothes, DVD players, kitchen tables, and anything else that's not directly or indirectly permanently attached to land.

The good thing about real estate is that you can touch it. If you have the address you can drive by and see what type of condition the property is in without having to be a real estate genius. On the other hand, if you are not financially literate in advanced finance concepts, trying to figure out if a stock or company is in good shape can be almost impossible.

Banks understand this very well and is one of the main reasons that they won't hesitate to give someone with a good credit and employment background all the money they need for a real estate investment, but will look at the same A credit borrower crazy if he or she came in asking for a loan of any size to buy stocks with.

This isn't meant to be a bashing of stocks because like I said, stocks can be a very valuable piece to a solid portfolio. My purpose is to separate and put a magnifying glass on the two and show the large difference in benefits between them. Investing in real estate has an enormous advantage over investing in stocks, and I feel this is one of the many things that you must know about real estate.

Buying Your First Home: The Basics

Buying your first home can be a very challenging and mentally draining experience. This is of course, if you aren't aware ahead of time of everything that is required of you and everything that you will be forced to go through in order to complete the process.

However, it is an experience that you should be happy to go through, as it is one of the best ways to build wealth in this country, as the net worth of a homeowner is usually 7 to 10 times higher than a non homeowner.

This is because when a home increases in value as it usually does, it creates equity for the homeowner. Equity is the difference between what it is worth and what you owe the mortgage lender. For example, let's say you have a home that is now worth $200,000 and you owe the mortgage lender $150,000. The $50,000 difference from the $200k it's worth and $150k you owe is considered equity, and that is your portion of "real ownership" in the home.

When a person sells a home, after the mortgage lender is paid off, whatever money remains belongs to the seller/previous owner of the home and it doesn't need to be shared with anyone, not even the bank that may have borrower them 100% of the money to purchase the home.

Generally in any business agreement, when someone provides the startup money of any amount, it is generally expected for that investor to receive a percentage of the profits, but in real estate that expectation doesn't exist. Real estate by far is the best investment out there, especially when all things are considered.

Before you start looking to buy your first home, it is important to make sure that your credit in intact. The better your credit, the lower the interest rate you will qualify for, so this is very important as it can save you tens of thousands of dollars over the life of the loan.

This doesn't mean that you must have perfect credit, it just means that you should make sure during the last 12 to 24 months leading up to your home purchase, that you don't have any 30 day late payments on any of your lines of credit that appear on your credit report.

If a person is late by 10 or 15 days on a credit account, it doesn't usually hurt their credit report, as your report only shows blemishes for payments that are not paid at all or for those that were paid greater than 30 days late.

Lines of credit that generally report monthly to the credit bureaus would include mortgages, car loans, credit cards, student loans, and any other revolving or installment credit you may have. Generally, the electric, gas and water companies do not report to the credit agency unless you become so delinquent that your account is sent to collections, which also isn't good if you are looking to buy a house soon.

Once you've done a good job in securing a good credit profile, it is wise to start shopping for the best mortgage lender for your situation. It is important to know that all lenders are not created equal, thus it is important to do your due diligence and find the best one for your particular situation. One lender may have a better program for perfect credit, while the other may have the best program for fair or good credit.

In the process of shopping for a loan, it is important to know your credit score ahead of time, so when companies give you quotes they don't have to pull your credit, which knocks your score down a few points with each pull.

Once you find a lender that you are comfortable with, you should ask to be pre approved so you can know how much of a home you can actually afford. After you get pre-approved you should then find a good realtor in your local area.

It is very important **not** to find a realtor before you find a lender, because most realtors are notorious for preferring you to their business sharing mortgage buddy down the street that may not be in your best interest.

In my opinion, 95% of all realtors have a mortgage lender who they trade business with, even if they know that the homebuyer could get a much better deal elsewhere. In return they expect their mortgage buddy to refer them all business that goes to them first, which isn't as bad because you as the homebuyer don't pay the realtor anyway.

Your realtor is paid from the commission that the seller agreed to pay his or her realtor when they listed their home for sale. The way it works is, if your agent brings you, as a buyer to the seller, than the commission that would've went solely to the selling agent is now split between the two agents 50/50.

The average selling realtor's commission ranges from 5 to 7% depending on how good the realtor is and how hard he or she believes it will be to sell the home. To give you a clearer picture of how this works, let's say a realtor's commission is 6% and the selling price is $200,000. The total commission for selling this house would be $12,000. If two agents are involved (buyer's and seller's agent) then the $12,000 commission would be split between the two agents 50/50 paying each agent $6,000.

Once you find a good realtor that you are comfortable with, you can start looking for a home. It is of the essence that you like the realtor that you choose, as you will be spending a lot of time with them riding around looking at houses. In many cases your realtor will become your temporary best friend, as you will begin to see them day and night, with phone conversations and emails between you and the realtor seeming routine until you find your home.

While looking at various homes, it is a good idea to visit the area at different times during the day to get a good feel for the true identity of the neighborhood. While visiting the neighborhoods it is always a good idea to knock on doors and ask questions about the neighborhood.

From my past experience, most of the elderly neighbors will be more than willing to tell you everything they know about the neighborhood, which will generally be some very helpful information for you and help you to decide if this is an area that you really want to live in.

Once you find a home that you are interested in, you and your realtor would then prepare an offer for the home. Most offers are made with several common contingencies to protect the potential buyer: Contingent upon financing, appraisal exceeding purchase price, and inspection being approved by buyer within 10 days.

Generally, a good realtor will have an inside scoop on what the bottom line is that the seller is willing to accept for their home. They usually get this information from the seller's agent, as they will both do all that they can to work together and sell the home.

This can be seen as very disloyal as a seller is under the impression that everything that they discuss in secrecy with their agent is kept confidential between them and their agent. This is generally not the case as both agents will share information with each other from the seller's agent telling the bottom line that the seller will take for the home and the buyer's agent will generally share the maximum dollar amount that the buyer is willing to pay for a particular property.

With that said, please don't expect anyone in a real estate transaction to be entirely on your side, not even yourself. If a person doesn't have their emotions in check before going into a real estate transaction, their emotions will normally effect the buying decision, thus leading an otherwise normally logical person to make an emotion based irrational decision.

When making an offer on a home, it is best to offer slightly under what your realtor has told you is the seller's bottom line, while at the same time asking the seller to pay some of your closing cost. In most states the seller is allowed to pay 3% of the purchase price for the buyers closing cost.

For example, if the listing price is $265,000 and your realtor told you that the seller's bottom line is $240,000, than you should offer $230,000 with the seller paying $6900 in your closing cost.

In many cases the seller will accept this offer, as it is close to what they wanted, and on top of that, their realtor will put a little pressure on them to do so. At this point either the seller will accept, reject or make a counter offer.

If the seller rejects your offer, than you can make another offer closer to what they are asking for the home in hopes that they will accept. If they make a counter offer, they will generally ask for more money and in most cases the two parties will find a way to meet in the middle.

In any case, once you have a contract/purchase and sell agreement is when the ball starts rolling. At this point you would order an inspection and then approve or disapprove what the report revealed. Generally, no inspection report comes back perfect, and whatever flaws that are found can be used to your advantage to negotiate a lower price on the home.

After all the final kinks are worked out with the inspection report, you then contact your mortgage lender and let them know that you have a purchase and sell agreement on a home. At this time you would complete an application online or over the phone and you will lock in an interest rate and closing cost.

Depending on the level of documentation that you will need to go (will be discussed in the mortgage chapter) you will then need to send in verification of pay stubs, bank statements, W2's, and potentially any other income or asset verification needed. You will also be required to sign some mortgage disclosures that include a Good Faith Estimate (GFE) and a Truth In Lending Statement.

After all of this information is received by the lender, they will generally order the appraisal for your home. The appraiser will do research on similar homes that have sold in the area of the home you're buying, as well as examine your home to come up with an approximate value of the home.

This process usually goes smooth, but in some cases you may find out that the seller is overcharging for their home and the appraised value may come back less than what you are paying for it. In most situations the lender will not be willing fund the mortgage for this home especially if it's 100% financing. You will be forced to renegotiate the purchase price of the home.

If the seller is not willing to renegotiate than it is usually a deal breaker, but in most cases the sellers are reasonable and will do what they need to do to sell the home.

Simultaneously, while the appraisal has been ordered, the mortgage company will order your title work to make sure that the sellers are the actual legal owners of the home. Also, the mortgage company will do an employment verification to make sure you're actively employed as you stated in your application.

If all of this information comes back fine, then your file will be submitted for underwriting. The underwriter will double check everything in the file and give a last say of yes or no or in some cases they will say yes upon certain conditions. A common condition may be that the buyer has to pay off certain collection accounts before closing. Whatever the case, after final approval from the underwriter, the file is sent to the closing department and the date and time of your closing is scheduled.

One of the last things that you must perform before closing is set up your homeowners insurance. Generally, you will have to pay one year worth of insurance upfront with your insurance company, which usually cost between $400 and $800 depending on the size and value of the home.

One thing I do recommend though is using the same company that you have your car insurance with, as they will normally give you a sizeable discount on both for doing so.

The closing is the final stage in the home buying process and can sometimes be the most mentally draining and demanding. At closing, you will often meet the sellers of the home unless they signed ahead of time. This is also where you literally get to read and sign over 50 forms.

It is very important to make sure that the interest rates and closing cost that you agreed to with your mortgage lender is what you are signing for at closing. It is very normal for the lender to offer you a good rate and low closing cost in order to win your business and then switch them both on you at closing.

If this happens to you, I recommend walking away from the closing table without signing anything. This is what the mortgage industry calls the "Bait and Switch". Don't go for it, as this is very unethical and deserves to be walked away from.

On the other hand, if everything is as agreed to, then you will literally spend hours reviewing and signing papers before finally being handed keys to your new home. At this point you are now considered a homeowner and can begin receiving the benefits of homeownership that are plentiful.

Although this may have been a long tiring process, it is definitely worth it. Once you go to your new home, it is always good to introduce yourself to all of your new neighbors especially those that are right next to you.

Investing In Real Estate

As I stated before, real estate is my favorite investment by far. No other investment out there has the benefits of real estate or even comes close for that matter. There are many ways to begin a career investing in real estate, and there are many different types of properties that a person can invest in.

The most common investment is in residential real estate. Generally when a person takes this route they buy single family or two family homes to begin with and then moves up as their experience and financial situation gets better.

The best way to teach you how this works will be to illustrate a scenario of a person who begins a career investing in real estate. I will walk you through as she moves from one property to the next using some very good techniques to get the absolute best mortgage possible.

The story I'm going to walk you through is the story of a woman named Michelle. When Michelle graduated from Spellman College in Atlanta, GA, with a double major in Business and Communications, she immediately got a job at a large fortune 500 company as the Asst. Sales Director that had a large office in downtown Atlanta.

Her new job came with a comfortable salary of $50,000 and chance for a yearly bonus of between $5,000 and $25,000 depending on the performance of her department that she oversaw. Being a hard worker for Michelle was inherent, so she new she could motivate her team to the highest level possible, and then of course receive the highest bonus possible.

After saving money to build a security nest for six months, she purchased her first home that was a 3 bedroom, 2 bath, 2 car garage home, 10 minutes from downtown Atlanta for $135,000. She bought the home with no money down, and got a pretty good mortgage since she let the mortgage lender know that she intended to "owner occupy" the home.

Her total PITI (principle, interest, taxes, and insurance) payment was only $1,025 that left her with plenty of extra cash each month to save for her next investment. Although she liked this home a lot, she didn't plan on living in it for long and she wanted to turn it into an investment/rental property and move up to a slightly bigger house to live in.

After six months of living in her first home she hired a real estate agent to help her find her next home to buy that she was going to live in. Her realtor told advised her that the best way to turn her current home into an investment/rental property would be to hire a reputable property management company.

She informed her that for a small percentage of rents collected, that the property management company would collect rents, pay any bills related to the property, handle any evictions if needed, and schedule all maintenance and repairs. She thought this was a good idea as she thought that the downside to investing in real estate was going to be receiving calls at 3 am about the hot water heater not working.

Using a property management company erased that concern as well as increased her chances of collecting rents on time each month, as tenants are more likely to pay a company on time than they would a person (the home owner) that they might not even like.

After hiring a property management company to take care of the property, she focused solely on finding her next home that would ultimately become an investment one day.

After looking for about 3 weeks, Michelle had a purchase and sale agreement on a nice home about 15 minutes from downtown Atlanta for $155,000. The home had 3 bedrooms, 2.5 bathrooms, and a 2 car garage, very similar to her first home. In addition to the three normal conditions in the contract (conditioned upon financing, appraisal, and inspection), she also added a condition that stated that her current home needed to be rented out with a 1 year lease before closing. This covered her end as she didn't want to be stuck paying two mortgages.

She hired a very good property management company that was able to rent out her current home approximately 3 weeks before closing on her new home. The rent being charged for her home was $1150, which was enough to cover PITI as well as the 8% charge to cover property management fees, so she was in pretty good shape to move forward.

After she closed on her new home, she became very excited about how the real estate business worked and made a commitment to find her next home within 3 months from the day of closing on her second home.

About 6 weeks after moving into her new home, she hired her current property management company to find a tenant for her current home, as she was ready to make her next move up and buy her third property.

Before Michelle had a chance to call the realtor good, the property management company already had a qualified tenant whom was ready to move in within 30 days. This caused Michelle and her agent to speed things up and look for that next property with extreme urgency.

Due to working with Michelle on her two prior home purchases, her realtor had a good idea of what type of home she wanted and they found their next home in 7 days. Purchasing this home didn't go as smooth as the other two as her mortgage guy told her that her "debt to income" ratio was getting too high and that in order for her to go full documentation and get the best rates possible, she would have to keep the mortgage under $140,000.

This is where the second problem came in at. The mortgage lender told her that by her buying a property that was worth less than her current home, the underwriter would automatically assume that this was an investment property, as there was no good logical reason for her to step down in home sizes except for one.

Her mortgage guy told her that the only logical excuse that the underwriter was likely to accept was that the third home that she was going to buy was going to be closer to her employer than her current home.

So this meant that Michelle would be forced to buy a home that was closer to her job, than her current home was, or she would be forced to get the mortgage based on an investment property, that would have a much higher interest rate and closing cost. She didn't want to pay investment property rates and did the smart thing and found a home that was about 5 minutes closer to her employer then her current home was.

After she bought her third home she decided to put a hold to her real estate purchases and wanted to grow some equity in her current homes so she could sell and move on to bigger and better investments.

She stayed still for about 2 years as she watched her property values dramatically increase. Purchasing homes so close to downtown really paid off, as after two years her first home that she paid $135,000 for was now worth $180,000. The second home she bought for $155,000 was now worth $200,000, and the third home that she paid $140,000 was now worth $190,000.

All together she had over $140,000 worth of equity combined in her three homes. She decided to sell all three homes with the same realtor that she had purchased the homes with, who in return, gave her a discount and sold her homes for her at a partial rate of 4%.

Due to the areas being as hot as they were, all three homes sold within 4 months and gave Michelle over $125,000 after all fees and closing cost were paid. At each closing, Michelle's smile on her face became bigger and bigger as she knew that she was headed toward financial security.

Before she completed the sale and closed on her last home, she had a nice 3,000 square feet home that had 4 bedrooms, 3 baths, and a 3 car garage under contract for $300,000 that had a mortgage payment of just under $2,000 when combined with taxes and insurance.

She bought this home with no money down, and with plans on being in it for a while, as she now wanted to focus on larger residential real estate, specifically small to mid-size apartment buildings.

She first tried to get pre-approved for a commercial loan with her current loan officer, but he informed her that his company couldn't finance any buildings over four units and recommended her to a good commercial lender that he knew and previously sent past customers to.

Michelle had over $140,000 at the time she met with the commercial lender who was very impressed with her ability to build such a large nest egg only two and a half years after college.

After reviewing her credit and verifying her employment, the lender approved Michelle for a $500,000 commercial loan, as long as she put down a minimum of 10% of her own money at closing.

The lender then referred her to a good commercial real estate agent that he shares business with. The lender assured Michelle that the realtor would be able to get her top quality for her money, which he wasn't lying about.

The first building that the realtor showed Michelle was a 20 unit apartment building 10 minutes from downtown Atlanta. The building was appraised to be worth over $600,000, but the realtor knew the selling realtor and got the word on it before it officially became a listing.

The seller was willing to accept $525,000 for the property as long as Michelle could get financing lined up and close within 45 days. To his surprise, Michelle was already ahead of the game and had a pre-approval letter in her back pocket.

Michelle made a formal offer in writing for the $525,000 and the seller gladly accepted. Three days after they came to an agreement on the sale price, Michelle did the wise thing and had the property inspected. This was very expensive as the building had twenty units, but it was well worth the cost.

During the inspection, the inspector discovered several problems with the plumbing and electricity in several units, and estimated the repair to cost over $15,000. After hearing this news Michelle got excited as she knew that she could further use this information to her advantage.

After discussing her concerns of the inspection with the seller, she was able to do a final negotiation on the price and wound up getting the building for $490,000. She then put down 10%, which was only $49,000 and had approximately $12,000 in closing cost.

While signing her share of paper work at the closing table, Michelle couldn't stop smiling as she saw her net worth potentially raise another $125,000 in a matter of hours. This was a big move for her as the building brought in an average of $600 a unit for a total gross income of $12,000. Her mortgage on the property was less than $3,500 and after all expenses were paid, gave her a net monthly profit of slightly over $6,000.

She then used this income to pay for her current mortgage on the home that she was living in, as well as pay for a 2006 CLS 500 Mercedes Benz for $62,000 that had a monthly note of $1,300.

The income that she was receiving from her apartment building gave her more than enough income to support a very comfortable lifestyle, not including the solid income that she was getting with her current employer. At this point she was basically living off of assets and enjoying herself while doing so.

Although Michelle had put herself in a very good position financially, she wasn't close to satisfied as she went on to purchase three more apartment buildings in less than 2 years. Her financial situation became very comfortable as she was able to quit her job and attend graduate school at Cornell University in New York.

She was studying to get her MBA in Hotel Management as she wanted her next step to be in hotel ownership. She knew that in two years when she graduated that she would be able to sell some of her apartment buildings for very nice profits that could potentially work as a great down payment on a mid-level hotel.

While in school, Michelle was given the opportunity to work several internships at very reputable hotel franchises that gave her first hand experience in the hotel business. Since Michelle had a very nice income from her investments that she made back home, she didn't have to work and spent all of her time in graduate school studying and learning all she could about the hotel business.

After graduating with her MBA in Hotel Management from one of the top hospitality schools in the country, she was on a mission to take the Atlanta hotel scene by storm, as she sold 3 of her apartment buildings for a profit of $575,000. With the financial condition that she was in, as well as her internationally respected MBA from Cornell in hotel management, Michelle had no problem getting approved for a $4,000,000 loan to purchase a very nice hotel.

The hotel that Michelle wound up buying was about 5 minutes from downtown Atlanta and had annual net profits of over $600,000. The price of the hotel was $3.7 million and required for Michelle to put down 10%, which was approximately $370,000 plus some cost to pay her broker in the transaction.

Although the income for her hotel was enough to live a very extravagant lifestyle, she maintained a very nice, yet modest living, only using revenue from the remaining apartment building that she had to live off of.

She kept this up for two years before she had over $1,000,000 in the bank. Of course not being the one to settle for less, Michelle purchased a second hotel about 20 minutes from downtown. This time she stepped it up a little and made the purchase at $7,000,000. She put 10% down once again, which was approximately $700,000, and this time is was well worth it, as the hotel had annual net profits of almost $2 million.

With an income of over $3 million annually she decided that it was time to sell her last apartment building, which she sold for a profit of $300,000. Life was great for Michelle as she went on to buy 2 more hotels within a 3 year period and raised her total income to over $7 million annually and her net worth to over $40 million before her 30th birthday.

Michelle was just an example of how one can gain a life of riches in the world of real estate investing if they're focused, and determined to provide a better life for themselves and their family.

Real Estate Investing In All Climates

Unlike the stock market, great real estate investments can be found year round no matter the economic season. During a trough, recovery, expansion, or peak, a great real estate investment can be found and profited from. There are several reasons why real estate can be good investment no matter the season for several reasons, but a couple in particular that I would like to cover are as follows.

1.) **Foreclosures on Adjusting Rate Mortgages:** Due to a never ending list of foreclosures, there are always under priced homes on the market that must sell, and in many cases, sell for approximately half of the appraised value. With the large use of ARM's (adjustable rate mortgages), more people than ever are falling victim to foreclosure as they can no longer make their mortgage payments once they adjust.

   In many scenarios, when rates were extremely low, people took out 3/1 and 5/1 ARM's (please see mortgage chapter for details) with 4% interest rates. Not having good sight or vision for the future, they ignored the form at closing that stated that their interest rates could jump as high as 9.75% at the first adjustment period, and another 1% annually until their interest reached a cap of 13%.

   This of course made a very large difference when the payment adjusted and became almost twice as high as it was originally. In some cases this causes the sellers to be put in a position to sell or be foreclosed upon, and with the credit effects of a foreclosure being close to deadly, a credit savvy home owner will do almost anything to avoid foreclosure.

   This type of situation is available for capitalization everyday, and is one of the main reasons why there are always good real estate investments around.

2.)   **YOU Don't Have To Pay The Mortgage:** One of my favorite traits of a good real estate investment is that the owner of the investment is rarely the one that ends up making the monthly mortgage payments. Generally, the mortgage and all other related expenses are paid by the tenant(s) of the property by way of rents collected by the owner or the property management company on the behalf of the owner. So with real estate it is common practice for the investor to borrow the money from the bank and let his or her tenants pay the money back, while the investment grows in value.

So even in a situation where properties aren't appreciating at a fast pace, an investor can still enjoy the benefits of equity by way of timely monthly payments from their tenants, thus making real estate an investment for all climates, even cold ones.

Spotting Good Investments

Spotting a good real estate investment can be a simple, yet challenging task at the same time. Depending on a person's investment philosophy (everyone needs one) a good investment could be determined by many different things.

In my opinion, a property that has the potential to increase in value steadily over a 3 to 5 year period, as well as has a strong enough rental market to have a tenant cover all related expenses to the property is a good one. Of course it has to fit within each individual investor's investment goals, but generally this is enough for a property to get my time and attention.

To make sure it meets these qualifications it is important to do a cash flow analysis that adds in detail all income from the property and subtracts from that all related expenses for the property as well as maintenance fees that may not truly in reality exist.

If after doing all of the required math and your gut still tell you that the subject property may make a good one, it is a good idea to do more due diligence and look at a history of home sales in the area to see how fast they have been appreciating over the last three to five years.

When looking at these numbers, it is important to remember that home values generally raise a lot faster in markets of low interest rates as we had over the past 4 years, as the demand for homes is a lot higher when mortgage interest rates are low.

As I said before, many things can make a good real estate investment all depending on the philosophy of the investor, as long as at the end of the day it makes a profit. "If it don't make dollars, than it don't make sense."

1031 Tax Deferred Exchange

The 1031 Tax deferred exchange is one of the best ideas that the IRS ever came up with in regards to doing something helpful for real estate investors. If used properly, the 1031 Exchange law can help a real estate investor become very rich in a much shorter time, than if the 1031 Exchange didn't exist.

What the 1031 Tax Deferred Exchange does, is give an investor the opportunity to sell a piece of property and put the total proceeds from the sale into another property without having to pay taxes on the gain or profit before doing so.

There are several stipulations/guidelines that must be adhered to in order to make this a success and they are listed as follows:

1.) The properties must be a "like kind" exchange. This means that the home sold and the new home that is being purchased must be similar to one another in reference to their use. For example, a home that was held for investment can only be exchanged for another home that is for investment. This could mean a single family home being traded for another single family home, or a single family home being traded for a 20 unit apartment building. As long as the properties have like kind use, than the 1031 Exchange can be applied.

2.) A new property must be identified within 45 days of the sale of the home where the profits have come from.

3.) The trade or exchange must take place and close within 180 days of the sale of the home where the profits have come from.

4.)   The proceeds must be held at a title company or bank that can act as an exchange bank. This means that you can't just deposit this money at your regular local bank without it acting as an exchange bank, and you definitely can't take the money home with you.

To give you a clear illustration of how the 1031 Tax Deferred exchange works, I'll give you the story of Jessica. Jessica was very beautiful and smart at the same time. She was mixed with Puerto Rican and Black, and had very long hair with gold streaks in it (for men who need visuals to stay attuned). On top of her beauty, she also had a Master's degree in Psychology that she earned in less than two years after completing her four year degree in business.

She had a lot on her side and she was determined to add wealth to that equation. She had a high paying job with a large oil company, but she was ready to live off of assets and spend her week days in the manner that she chose and work when she pleased.

After years saving money she purchased a $300,000 small 10 unit apartment building. Although she enjoyed the income that came in from the building on a monthly basis, she was ready to sell after 2 years as the property's value went from $300,000 to $525,000.

After selling the property, Jessica had net proceeds of $225,000 that she held at her local title company with the intentions to use to purchase a "like kind" property.

After two weeks (within the 45 day requirement) Jessica spotted a 20 unit apartment building that was selling for $750,000 and notified the title company that she had a property in mind.

After searching for another couple of weeks to see if she could find anything else that she wanted to put the money in (the proceeds for a 1031 exchange can go into more than one property as long as they are all "like kind"), she decided that she was going to put the entire $225,000 into her new building and closed within 75 days (within the 180 day requirement).

In this case, since Jessica used the 1031 exchange to perfection, she was able to avoid paying taxes on the $225,000 that she had gained from the sale of her original apartment building, which allowed her to put more money into a larger investment.

After holding this apartment building for 3 years, Jessica was again ready to sell as the value rose in value from $750,000 to $1.3 million.

In this case she was able to sell the property and gain a profit of over $550,000, which she again held at her local title company with the intentions of buying a "like kind" property.

This time around she found two properties that she wanted to invest in. Being allowed to do so, she invested half of the money into an upscale 18 unit building and the other half into a large 30 unit apartment building.

One important thing to note when exchanging properties is that you do eventually have to pay taxes at the end of the line (if there ever is an end) when you finally sell a property and want to take some cash out and use in a different way other than to purchase a "like kind" property.

Watching Jessica use her total profits to invest in another "like kind" property should give a good picture for how it works, and another idea on how you can make it a success for you.

Tax Benefits of Depreciation

Another great benefit with investing in real estate is the tax favor real estate investors receive. Although most homes don't depreciate in value, a real estate investor is allowed to depreciate an investment property over 27.5 years. This is a great benefit and usually makes most of the income received tax free.

The way depreciation works is, it's considered an expense that is deducted from the income that's received. For example, if an investment property had $3,000 worth of net income and $3,000 worth of depreciation, than the taxable income would be $0, thus causing $0 taxes being paid on the income from the property.

The way depreciation is calculated is by dividing the purchase price of the investment property (minus the land) by 27.5. For example, if an investment property (minus the land) cost $300,000, you would divide that by 27.5. That would give you $10,909 of depreciation that can be subtracted from the income for the property. If the net income was less than $10,999, than the income received on this property would be basically tax free.

This is a great benefit. The only slight downside is that this decreases your cost basis by the amount that is was depreciated by. This means that it creates a larger profit at the time of sale, but if using the 1031 exchange, this downside is basically irrelevant.

Using Property Management Companies

A good property management company can be a real estate investor's best friend, and in some cases can also be their worst enemy. A good property management company will fill any vacancies, collect all rents, mail your mortgage payments, perform any evictions (if necessary) and schedule any maintenance work that is required for the up keeping of the property.

Just as a restaurant manager makes sure that everything is intact at his or her establishment, so does a good property management company.

A good property management company will do extensive credit and background checks before putting someone into your property, and they will be very firm, yet professional and respectful about collecting rents on a timely basis.

A good property management company will save an investor from a million and one headaches, as the investor rarely ever (if ever) comes in contact or is introduced to the tenants. This means that at 3 am, if the hot water heater breaks down, instead of calling you, they will call the property manager. Also, if anything else is wrong or need taken care of, the property management company is where the buck stops as they won't even know you as the property owner.

Depending on the level of business you give a property management company, they will generally charge a management fee of 5 to 8% of the rents collected. They will also generally charge a fee for finding tenants that can range from a couple hundred dollars, to as much as the first months rent.

I find property management companies very useful as I'm not a good landlord, nor do I ever want to be one. One must be careful of scrupulous property management companies that will steal from you, so it is important that your property manager send you a monthly statement, and that you review it and question any discrepancies.

Flipping Real Estate

Although flipping real estate is probably considered more to be gambling than investing, I figured some of my readers would won't me to cover it, so I'll touch on the basics of the matter.

Flipping real estate involves purchasing a property for a low price and then quickly reselling the property at a profit. Sometimes the property is re-sold/assigned to a third party without the title ever being put in the investor's hands. Flipping can be done in many ways and I'll cover a couple to wrap up this chapter on real estate investing.

The two tactics that I'm going to cover are an outright purchase and then sell, and the other will be assigning a contract to a third party without ever taking possession of the property.

Purchase & Then Sell

This is probably the most common form of flip, as many houses are rehabbed first before being put back on the market to be resold. This is almost impossible to be done when assigning a contract, and very risky as well.

To give you a clear illustration on how this form of flipping would take place, I'll give you the story (without a description this time) of Mya.

Mya was looking for some fast income and was informed about the possible benefits of flipping real estate from a casual friend of hers. Under his direction, she had some signs made with statements such as "We Buy Homes Fast", and "Avoid Foreclosure".

The first day the signs were up, she got about 15 calls. Not all calls were quality as many people wanted full value for their homes, which left no room to profit from for Mya if she bought a home at full price.

Eventually, Mya got a call from a desperate seller that had lost her employment with a prestigious accounting firm and needed to sell badly in order to avoid foreclosure. During the first two minutes of the phone call, Mya wisely found out that the home was worth $180,000, and the lady owed $115,000, and was willing to take $125,000 for the property if Mya could purchase the home and close within 30 days.

Mya had excellent credit so she was able to get financing and she purchased the property and closed within the 30 day time frame. The home was in a great area, as it was located near some good schools, close to both shopping and highways.

Immediately Mya had the interior painted and did some other minor work that in all cost her around $2,000. At this point, Mya had $127,000 invested in the home. She didn't have any closing cost when she bought the home because she agreed to a no closing cost loan that came with a much higher interest rate. This was a good idea as she was only going to be keeping this home for a short period of time.

After having the work done, Mya had the home appraised and it came back at $190,000. She then put up ads in the newspaper as well as on Craigslist stating that she had a $190,000 property selling for only $160,000.

Within hours after the ads were posted, she received numerous phone calls from motivated buyers who began bidding on the home and the high demand allowed Mya to actually sell the home for $168,000 (Remember supply & demand. The demand was higher than the supply).

This gave Mya a quick profit of $41,000 that she was able to use the 1031 exchange with and buy another property to flip or hold as an investment, if that's what she wanted to do with the money.

This was just a simple example of flipping real estate after taking the title in your name, and can be used by anyone with a little ambition to be a successful real estate flipper (not investor).

There a couple potential downfalls of using this approach. Many mortgage lenders will not finance a home if the seller has not held title for a certain period of time. In some case the lender wants the title to be in the sellers name for a minimum of 60 days, and some may require 90 days. Not all mortgage companies have this requirement, but it is important to know exactly who you're doing business with, and to make sure the buyer of the home is willing to use a lender that doesn't have a title "seasoning" requirement.

Another potential downfall could be the value of the property decreasing before the seller has enough time to sale at a profit. This generally will not happen if you bought the home with a large enough gap (value of home vs. what you paid for it), as was the case with Mya, but it can still happen depending on many things including the neighborhood, or the condition of the economy.

If you buy the home at the peak of a business cycle when inflation is skyrocketing, this will cause the Federal Reserve to raise interest rates (to control inflation), and generally property values will decline if unattractive interest rates appear on the market.

In some cases, if the demand for housing is much higher than the supply, than high interest rates will not have as much of an effect on the value of homes, as people still need a place to sleep.

Flipping real estate can be very lucrative if done correctly. It can also be very dangerous if done incorrectly, so be careful when choosing properties to flip. Reading Rev Run's (from Run DMC) new book lately, I read a very important statement. "Learn to say no. The things you walk away from, determine the things you walk in to. So choose wisely".

Assigning Real Estate To A Third Party

Assigning real estate to a third party can either be an easy transaction, or on the flipside can become a nightmare in hell full of law suits and dead bodies (if you gansta' like that).

For the most part, I like to consider people as being good hearted people who spend most of their trying to be successful and don't really care about the next man (or woman) being successful as long as they're eating properly.

Sometimes in flipping real estate you learn that this not the case. Surprisingly, when some people find out that you are about to make a quick profit off of them, they turn into what I like to call "haters".

Even if their needs are being met in the transaction, some people (I assume because of the way they were raised) have a problem with yours being met, as if you are suppose to do business so everyone else profits except for you.

If you plan on assigning a real estate contract to someone, it is very important to notify everyone involved in writing from the beginning to help prevent any unnecessary law suits and legal headaches.

To now give you an illustration of flipping a property by assigning a contract, I'll give you the story of Kimberly.

One day while driving home from work she noticed a for sale sign on a beautiful two story home. She didn't have a chance at a mortgage because her credit was in drastic need of repair, so she knew she couldn't flip the property by purchasing it outright as she couldn't get financing.

When she made the offer on the property, she listed the buyer of the home as herself or "assignee". Already using her credit as a way out, because if she couldn't assign it to anyone, she also knew that she wouldn't be able to get financing so she could use the ability to get financing condition in the contract as a safe way out of the contract if needed.

Nevertheless, Kim was able to find a buyer that way willing to purchase the home for $10,000 more than Kim had it under contract for which gave her a quick and easy $10,000 profit at closing.

Of course Kim did the right thing and notified the new buyers immediately of what her plans were, and they were okay with it as they were able to get a home for 90% of its fair market value, which is the way it's supposed to be. Like Jay-Z said "if you balling; keep balling, if you hating; STOP!"

Summary of Chapter

Following the techniques and knowledge found in this chapter will put you in position to live very comfortably if that is what you desire, and at worst case scenario, you will at least be prepared to go through the battles of purchasing your first home.

Buying a home can be a very mind boggling task when unprepared, so at least I hope you now feel that you can tackle this process with no problem. Also if you never knew how to begin real estate investing, you should now know the basic steps to get started, and possibly end up in a very good lifestyle living off of assets like Michelle. For more information on real estate investing, visit www.BlackBusinessSmart.blogspot.com.

Chapter 4
What You Need To Know About Mortgages

With all the talk about real estate investing, it is important to note that in most cases without a mortgage, none of it would be possible. A mortgage is simply a loan for real property. The real property is generally the collateral for the loan.

In most cases a person doesn't have the ability to buy a home or apartment building outright with cash, and therefore a loan is required to do so. Depending on the situation of the borrower, this may be an easy or difficult process.

A mortgage is definitely considered a secured loan, as if the borrower defaults on the mortgage, the bank has the complete right and ability to repossess or foreclose on the home and then resell it in an attempt to get their money back.

Almost every bank provides mortgage loans, as the demand for mortgages has dramatically increased over the last 15 years as more families have discovered the benefits of home ownership and have decided to purchase a home.

In the past, unless a person had 20% down, they were denied mortgages as the banks considered this borrower to be of high risk. Nowadays, not only can a person get 100% financing for a home, some lenders will actually give 103% loans to help cover the closing cost.

This is a significant difference to the way mortgages were given in the past, as now practically anyone can be qualified for a mortgage with little or no money down. Nowadays, even a person with a bankruptcy can get a mortgage and in some cases as soon as one day out of bankruptcy.

Things have definitely changed for the better for prospective home buyers as they no longer have to jump through hoops to become homeowners.

Prime vs. Sub Prime

The mortgage a person or family can usually qualify for is divided into two categories: prime and sub prime. The difference of the two is usually tens or hundreds of thousands of dollars if both loans are held for the entire length of the loan.

The ideal situation of any potential homebuyer is to get their credit in order before buying a home so that they won't be faced with what some experts consider a predatory loan. However, many people will buy homes without getting their credit situation in good shape and therefore will be forced to take less than decent interest rates on their mortgage.

A prime loan is for someone with good credit that usually meets all guidelines set by government institutions Fannie Mae and Freddie Mac. In the past, prime loans were only given to people with credit scores in the high 700's. This has dramatically changed as programs allow borrowers with credit scores in the low to mid 600's to qualify for prime loans.

A prime loan generally has a very good interest rate, with no pre-payment penalties (will be discussed later in chapter), and very reasonable closing cost. Being in a position to qualify for a prime loan is the ideal situation, as it will save a borrower a ton of money, and not just over time, but also in the beginning stages of the loan process with closing cost.

On the flipside of things, a sub prime loan is for someone whose credit situation doesn't meet all Fannie and Freddie guidelines, and is generally just a "band-aid" loan, not intended to be held for the life of the loan.

A sub prime loan may go to someone who is recently coming out of a bankruptcy, foreclosure, or someone who has a bad past of not paying credit related bills on time, and their credit score may be in the high 500's to low 600's.

Someone being forced to borrower a sub prime loan, may also have many collection accounts on their credit report that they are unable to pay, in which most prime lenders require to be satisfied, prior to or at closing.

Generally a sub prime loan is meant to be kept for only two or three years, as it is meant to be refinanced after the borrower has had time to improve their credit by paying their mortgage and other debts on time during that period.

Depending on the credit situation of the borrower, a sub prime loan may have an interest rate of 13%, while the prime loan average is around 6%, which can make a huge difference in monthly payments.

Mortgages Based On Property Use

Not every mortgage is created equal as we will see throughout this chapter, and not every mortgage presents the same amount of risk to the lender. When a lender decides to borrow money to someone, the main objective of the lender in the process is to find out how much risk the particular borrower presents to the potential lender.

A portion of the risk level is determined by the borrower's intentions for the subject property. There are generally three uses for a property: primary residence, second home, and investment property.

The way the lender or mortgage industry for that matter determines the level of risk associated to each one is by thinking "which is the first to go". What this means is, the lender tries to use logic and figure out what type of property would be the first to go, or have payments stopped being made on them if a person owned all three (primary, second home & investment), and all income stopped coming in.

Investment Property

Of the three, an investment property is considered the first to go if all income stopped coming in, and therefore carries the most risk and has the highest interest rate and closing cost.

An investment property also usually has tenants that hardly ever treat the home with the same care that the homeowner would, thus adding an extra layer of risk that must be paid for by way of a higher interest rate and closing cost.

There are several ways to try and get around paying this premium if buying an investment property. The most common thing to do is list the home as a primary residence, with the "intentions" of moving into the home within 30 days after closing. If you know you are the type of person that changes your mind often, this is a good way to be honest about the situation, and still save money at the same time.

If you do decide to move into the home, there is no minimum amount of time that you have to live there to satisfy the owner occupancy requirement before you retreat to a previously owned home, or go off and buy a new one. To give you a clear illustration of how this works, I'm going to give you the story of Monica.

Monica was a business women living in New Jersey and working in New York, who was the owner of 2 condos in New Jersey. Monica liked living in New Jersey, but she wanted to invest in a new condo that was being built near her place of employment in lower Manhattan.

When she went online to get mortgage rates, she discovered that marking the home as an investment property vs. a primary residence or second home would cost her an extra several thousand dollars and a 2% higher interest rate.

As she set at the computer she wondered how she could get the primary residence rates, while still being honest about the situation (she recently confessed Christ and was trying to live right). She was curious about how long she would have to stay in the home to for fill the owner occupancy requirement, so she called the 800 number and spoke to one of the loan representatives.

He informed her that as long as she had the "intentions" to move in to the home and make it her primary residence within 30 days, that it would be eligible for primary residence rates and cost. He also informed her that after she moved in to the home, that there was no minimum on how long she had to remain a primary resident of that home.

She knew that this meant that she could move into the home for a month or two and move out and back into one of her condos in New Jersey. Then she could turn it into an investment property by renting it out to a tenant, while keeping her primary residence rate and cost mortgage.

She took heed to this information and purchased the home as her primary residence. Instead of moving of all of her things from New Jersey, she packed some of her cloths, and bought an air mattress and lived at the home for about a month, before renting it out and going back to her condo in New Jersey.

Second Home

A second home presents the second highest amount of risk and therefore has cost and interest rates that are higher than that of a primary residence, while lower than that of an investment property. A second home is usually far away from a person's primary residence and may even be on beach, such as a condo overseeing the waters in Miami.

Generally there is not a big difference in pricing between a primary residence and a second home, and depending on the lender, pricing may be the same. One thing a lender won't tolerate is a borrower purchasing a home 10 miles away from their current home and trying to label it as a second home.

The mortgage company is going to automatically assume that this is going to be an investment property because of how close it is. The logic behind it is that, a reasonable person would not purchase a second home only a few minutes away from their primary residence as a second home is usually used for vacation or some type of getaway.

If you are buying a property that you want listed as a second home, depending on the lender, it must be at 120 miles away from your primary residence. If for some reason you are not in a position to for fill this requirement, following the footsteps of Monica is always available.

Primary Residence

A person's primary residence is considered the place where they intend to sleep, eat, and use the restroom on a consistent basis. As mentioned before, a home being purchased as a primary residence has the best rates and cost available to a potential borrower.

This is because a primary residence is considered to have the least amount of risk, as a home owner living in their own property is likely to oversee and take good care of the property. Also, if a person owned three houses: a primary residence, a second home, and an investment property and all income stopped coming in, the likely reaction of a reasonable person is to do all they can to make payments on their primary residence as that is where they live and shelter their family.

It is important to note that it is totally legal and ethical to purchase a chain of homes one after another, listing them as your primary residence, and after moving in them for a short period of time, renting them out and going on to purchase the next home. This can be done while listing them all as your intended primary residence at the time of the mortgage application, as long as you really intend to make the home your primary residence within 30 days after closing.

Criteria For Getting A Mortgage

If a person has done all the leg work to getting their credit situation in order, the mortgage qualifying process is generally full of choices more than limitations, as someone with excellent credit can buy a home without having employment if they meet certain criteria.

The mortgage qualifying process considers three things in order of importance: credit score, debt to income ratio (often referred to as "DTI"), and assets. Although all three of these items come in to play when looking for a conventional mortgage, the latter two can be disregarded for certain types of prime mortgages.

However, it is important to note that when looking for a conventional prime mortgage, it is important to have all three intact, as all three will be considered if you are applying for a full documentation (will be discussed later in chapter) loan that comes with the best interest rates and closing cost.

Credit Criteria

A person's credit score is the only function of the three that is considered with generally all types of loans available, thus making it the most important factor. There are loans that will be discussed in detail later in this chapter, that can be given with no regard to income, employment (if any exist), and if a person has sufficient assets to appear as a financially stable borrower.

As the most important factor, the first thing that a lender looks at is a person's credit history. If the score is excellent, the lender knows that even if the borrower's employment history is poor or even non-existent for that matter, that there are still products/mortgages available.

On the flip side of things, if a person's credit history is horrible, there is little to nothing that can be done to compensate for this situation, even if the borrower has 20 years of continuous employment with the same company, and has a $1 million salary.

The credit situation of a home buyer can be compared to the driving situation of an everyday person. If the person that is driving has a drivers license, but one of his tail light are cracked or no longer working, and the police pulls him over, although this is a slight problem and a violation of most city or state ordinances, the police officer may just give him a warning and let him continue to drive.

In this situation I'm basically saying that if your credit is good, but some of the other factors are poor or even non-existent, there are programs that can be used to compensate for this negative, in order to allow the borrower to still qualify for a good prime loan.

On the other hand, if the driver is driving without a driver license, but has a car that is in perfect condition and the police pull him over, he is generally going to be ticketed and have his car towed. In this situation, even though no headlights or rearview mirrors are damaged, because the driver is lacking the most important thing, he is disqualified from being allowed to drive.

This is very comparable to the credit situation of a borrower. A person can have a great job with all the benefits in the world, and have thousands or even millions of dollars in their bank account, but if their credit situation is horrible, it generally will disqualify them from getting approved for any type of mortgage.

As told to me by one of my business professors in college, "credit is the most important thing, so guard it with your life".

Debt To Income ("DTI") Criteria

The debt to income ratio, also known as "DTI" of a person is very important when applying for a conventional prime mortgage. The debt to income ratio measures the level of debt of a borrower compared to their level of income.

The debt to income ratio of a person is calculated by adding up all of a person's debt as it appears in monthly payments on a person's credit report and dividing it by the gross monthly income of the borrower(s). To give you a clear example of how this works, I will give you the story of Jasmine.

Jasmine was looking to buy a home, and had spent the last two years doing all that she could to get her credit in tip top shape. She knew that her credit was good, but now had to figure out how much money she could afford to borrow for a conventional, full documentation mortgage that has the best interest rates and closing cost.

When she called her loan officer at the local bank, after seeing that she had great credit, he told her that he would need to calculate her DTI to figure how much of a home she could buy, without having to use an unconventional mortgage that would have higher interest rates and closing cost.

Because he's a salesman first, and a loan consultant second, he invited her down to the bank so he could go over some things with her, and ultimately sell her a loan, since she had A-1 credit.

The loan officer told her that there was two ways to figure out her DTI and he wanted to share both ways with her for her own knowledge, which would then make his job easier, as he wouldn't have to answer constant questions about "what if my payment what this…..would that be too much?"

The first way was to add up all of her minimum monthly payments from debt listed on her credit report. On her credit report she had a car loan that had a monthly payment of $250, three student loans totaling $200 a month, and a credit card with a $30 minimum payment. This put her total monthly debt at roughly $480 a month.

They assumed that her mortgage payment including taxes and insurance would be roughly $1200. This then put her total monthly debt at $1680. Her gross monthly income from her employment was $3,500 on a $42,000 annual salary. To calculate her DTI, they divided the total monthly debt of $1680 by her monthly gross income of $3,500, and calculated a debt to income ratio of 48% (1,680/3,500).

He told her that with most prime loans that they needed to keep their DTI no higher than 50% to make it through underwriting, so she shouldn't choose a home that has a higher monthly payment than the $1200 they used to calculate her DTI. She understood, so of course she agreed, and then asked for him to show her the other way to calculate her DTI.

He told her that the other way didn't exactly calculate her DTI, but what it does is assumes a certain DTI goal, and then tells you the maximum monthly payment or total debt you can have to stay under that stated goal.

She was slightly confused, so he pulled out a clean piece of paper and starting showing her the exact math formula he was speaking about. He told her that if she wanted to keep her DTI under 50%, she would take her gross monthly income, which was $3,500 and multiply it by .5, which actually cuts it in half to $1750.

He told her that the $1750 represented the total amount of debt that she could have as far as minimum monthly payments in order to keep her DTI under 50% or .5. He then told her that she needed to subtract all current debt as shown on her credit report, which was her car payment of $250, her student loans of $200, and her credit card payment of $30.

After subtracting all of her debt from the $1,750 maximum figure, she was left with $1270 that represented what could be spent on her new home's mortgage payment.

So basically what she did was take her monthly gross income of $3,500 and multiplied it by the desired debt to income ratio (in this case 50% or .5), which came out to $1,750. They then subtracted all of her current debt that was listed on her credit report from the $1,750 number. The amount that was remaining came out to be $1,270, which represented the amount that could be spent on a monthly mortgage payment, while keeping her debt to income ratio under 50%.

As stated earlier, the debt to income ratio of a person is very important when applying for a full documentation loan, and just like your credit situation, must be intact and kept under certain limits depending on your credit score to be approved.

Assets Criteria

Generally of all three, the assets section isn't as important as the guidelines are generally easy to meet for someone with a good income and saving history. Also if a rational (one who uses logic and valid reasoning) person has been preparing themselves to purchase a home, then they would normally save up money for a down payment and closing cost.

When being qualified for a full documentation loan, the lender wants to make sure that you have the necessary funds to close, which generally includes your down payment (if any), closing cost, and several months of reserves. Reserves refer to money that will be remaining in your bank account or liquid investment accounts after closing.

Most lenders require at least two to six months of mortgage payments in reserves after closing. This is considered a security cushion in case the borrower has a glitch in employment or falls upon hard times.

In the case of such events, the lender would hate for the borrower to default on the loan because they didn't have any savings, and then have to foreclose on the property and try to resell it to get their money back.

Most lenders also require that the assets for closing as well as any reserves be "seasoned". This means that they want to see that the money has been there (in the account), or at least building for the last two to three months.

This is because, if given the opportunity, some people who don't have any reserves, would just borrow money from a friend or family member and place it in their bank account so it shows on their statement, and then take the money right back out and give it back to the person whom they borrowed it from, thus leaving the borrower with no reserves in actuality.

Although the assets criteria is important when applying for a full documentation loan, it is one of the criteria that can be disregarded when using certain unconventional products for home financing.

In summary of the criteria for getting a mortgage approved, credit is king (or in chess the queen) and the debt to income ratio and asset requirements are similar to the pawn and can be easily replaced, thus are expendable.

Levels Of Documentation Available

When applying for a mortgage, there are various levels of documentation you can choose to provide. These choices exist for various reasons, and some are even created to target certain types of people.

Each level of documentation has its' own level of risk, and generally comes with its own interest rate and closing cost. Also, the riskier the loan product, the harder it is to qualify for it as the credit requirement increases with each step down.

In case I haven't made this point clear, the more risk a lender assumes by borrowing a particular person money to buy a home, the more they will charge by way of interest rates and closing cost to compensate for that risk.

The levels of documentation that I'm going to discuss in detail from the least to the most amount risk for the lender are full documentation, stated income, no ratio, stated income stated assets (SISA), no income no assets (NINA) and No Documentation.

Full Documentation

A full documentation loan is considered conventional. It is the standard level of documentation across the board, and comes with the best interest rates and closing cost.

When applying for a full documentation loan you must provide current pay stubs, the last two years of W2's, bank statements, investment account statements (if that's were your down payment or closing cost is coming from), and the lender will have the company that you work for verify your employment.

As the name describes, you must provide the lender with full documentation of practically everything you stated in your loan application.

When applying for a full documentation loan, the lender will consider and verify your credit, debt to income ratio, as well as assets available for closing and reserves. If the home that you are buying puts your debt to income ratio at 65%, than the lender is going to tell you to either find a different home, or try a different level of documentation that will offset this high DTI.

Also if your liquid assets that you can document are not enough to meet the reserve requirement or even the down payment or closing cost for that matter, the lender will likely tell you to save up more money before looking to buy a home, or in a case where the borrower thinks they can come up with the cash to close, the lender may refer them to a different product where assets do not need to be verified before closing.

So with full documentation, the borrower needs to have a reasonable income comparable to the loan amount to keep the DTI under 50%, seasoned assets for down payment (if any), closing cost and reserves, and of course the "queen" must be still on the board, thus the borrower needs to have a credit history that meets Fannie Mae and Freddie Mac guidelines.

It is important to note that full documentation is available for both prime and sub prime loans, as most of the levels of documentation are only available for prime loans.

Stated Income

Stated income is the next step down in case a person can't qualify for a full documentation loan due to a debt to income ratio that exceeds the lender's maximum limits.

With stated income, a borrower would have to write a letter "stating" an income. This income can be any amount as long as it is reasonable for the occupation of the person. Generally the income stated will be just enough to meet the debt to income ratio requirements.

In addition to providing the letter of stated income, when using stated income as your level of documentation, you will have to be employed in the same field of work for a minimum of two years consecutively, and would still have to verify "seasoned" assets for closing and reserve requirements.

This program is regularly used by self employed people as they normally have a large number of tax write offs and a depleted adjusted gross income. In the case of a self employed person using stated income, they would have to provide a copy of their business license for the last two years or a CPA (certified public account) letter stating that they have been doing the self employed person's taxes for the previous two years, as it is a requirement to be self employed for a minimum of two years in order to go stated documentation.

As is the case with full documentation, stated income can be used for prime and sub prime loans, and comes with a slightly higher interest rate and closing cost than when using full documentation.

No Ratio

Taking a step down from stated income, no ratio is the third riskiest level of documentation, and thus has the third highest interest rate and closing cost. A person would generally use no ratio if their debt to income ratio was too high, and because of the occupation of the borrower, they couldn't state enough income without it being unreasonable for the occupation.

With no ratio, a person's debt to income ratio is no longer considered, thus taking away one-third of the potential headache with qualifying for a mortgage loan. When using no ratio, a person's employment is still verified, and they must prove that they have been in the same line of work for at least two years consecutively, but like I said the person's income isn't inquired about, as it is irrelevant when going no ratio.

Similar to stated income, all self employed persons must prove that they have been self employed for a minimum of two years, and must provide either a copy of the business license for the last two years, or a letter from a CPA stating that they have prepared the business's taxes for the last two years.

It is important to know that no ratio level of documentation is only available for prime loans and can't be used for sub prime loans, as is the case with full documentation and stated income.

Also, as with stated income, a persons assets must be verified though bank statements and investment account statements depending on where the money for down payment and closing cost are coming from.

Stated Income, Stated Assets

A step down further from no ratio is stated income, stated assets, which is also known as "SISA". With stated income, stated assets, a borrower would have to write a letter stating what their income and assets are.

This is normally done by someone, whose income and liquid assets are not enough to meet debt to income ratio and reserve requirements. With "SISA", a person still needs to be employed for a two year minimum in the same field, but the difference from the other programs, is that neither income nor assets are verified.

Stated income, stated assets is another loan that is only available with prime loans, and is not available with sub prime loans. Also it is important to note, that just as is the case with stated income, when using stated income, stated assets, the income stated for the borrower needs to be reasonable for their occupation.

No Income, No Assets

The next level down would be no income, no assets, which is also known as "NINA". No income, no assets is very similar to stated income, stated assets in the context that neither income nor assets are verified.

The difference is that with NINA, the borrower's income isn't inquired about, nor is their assets. In this case, a borrower wouldn't even have to state what their income or assets are as with stated income, stated assets. With NINA, no one cares.

However, as is the case with every other loan up until this point, your employment will be verified when going no income, no assets, and must have two years of continuous employment in the same line of work.

This is another loan that is only available for prime borrowers, and is not available with any sub prime loans.

No Documentation

The last step on the way down is where you will find no documentation. As the riskiest level of documentation, it also has the highest interest rate and closing cost. The only thing that is considered when applying for a no documentation loan is the borrower's credit history.

With no documentation, there are no questions asked about a person's employment situation, or about their financial situation, as it isn't asked about, and therefore it isn't provided. Because no questions are asked about this loan, it is often used by wealthy unemployed people, and in some scenarios, pimps and drug dealers with good credit who want t to purchase a home.

There's not any investigation into the borrowers employment past or anything. The borrower could be fresh out of jail for all the lender cares to know, after doing ten years on drug charges, and with the money he had stashed away is now deciding to settle down and buy a house or investment property.

So with no documentation, as long as the borrower has excellent credit, they are okay, and don't need employment nor do they need to have any money in the bank.

Types of Mortgages

When deciding on an actual mortgage product, a borrower has a lot of options to choose from based on what their needs are. Although there are possibly more mortgage products available than I can care to know, I will cover the most popular types with you that include fixed, adjustable, interest only, balloons, and pay option arms, which are also known as negative amortization loans.

When deciding on a mortgage product, a person needs to have an idea of how long they plan on keeping the property, likely rate of appreciation in the area, and if they're income will adjust throughout the length of the loan.

After a person or family successfully answers all of these questions, they should be able to pick the right mortgage product for themselves that addresses their needs, and at the lowest cost possible. Here's a description of the most popular types of loans.

Fixed Rate Mortgage

A fixed rate mortgage is a mortgage where the interest rate and monthly payments stay the same for the duration of the loan. If a person plans on staying in a home for a long time or isn't sure about how long they'll stay in a home, I would always recommend going with a fixed rate mortgage, as it's always better to be safe than sorry.

The most popular fixed rates mortgages on the market in order of popularity are 30 year fixed, 15 year fixed, and the recent creation of the 40 year fixed.

30 Year Fixed Mortgage

With a 30 year fixed mortgage, the amount borrowed is amortized (paid off) over 30 years. The interest that the money is financed at stays the same (fixed) for the entire 30 years. During that 30 year period, the monthly mortgage payment stays the same, thus making it a fixed mortgage.

If the borrower makes extra payments toward the principle throughout the life of the loan, the monthly payment would still remain the same, and the only adjustment that would be made is to the number of payments that need to be made. This would of course shorten the life of the loan depending on how much extra is paid to the principle.

A 30 year fixed mortgage is generally more expensive than many of the other products as the interest rate is fixed for 30 years, offering the borrower security from interest rate increases. Another reason for the higher cost is the ability to slowly pay back the loan over a 30 year period at the same low rate.

15 Year Fixed

A 15 year fixed mortgage is amortized (paid off) over 15 years, and generally comes with a lower interest rate and lower closing cost than that of a 30 year fixed, as you're paying the money back in half the time.

This mortgage is generally for someone who has enough income to afford the higher payments that would come with paying the mortgage off in half the time of a 30 year mortgage, as well as someone who doesn't want to be tied to a mortgage for 30 years.

Although with a 15 year fixed mortgage, you are paying the mortgage off in half the time of a 30 year fixed, the mortgage payment is only approximately a 40 to 50% increase, versus double as many would think since you're cutting the length of the mortgage in half.

I actually like the 15 year fixed, especially for someone that can afford the slightly higher payments. I also like the fact of being able to own the property outright in 15 years, versus in 30 years, which can seem like a lifetime to some people.

40 Year Fixed Mortgage

The recent emergence of the 40 year fixed has allowed many families in certain areas of the country to afford homes when they would otherwise not be able to. As the name indicates, a 40 year fixed mortgage is amortized (paid off) over 40 years and generally has higher closing cost and interest rates than a 30 and 15 year fixed as you're borrowing the money for a longer period of time.

The 40 year fixed slightly has a lower payment of maybe 10 to 15% less than a 30 year fixed, which may sound small, but does wonders for many families living paycheck to paycheck.

Other fixed products do exist such as the 20 and 10 year fixed and are priced accordingly using the same logic that's used on pricing the other fixed products.

Adjustable Rate Mortgage

An adjustable rate mortgage is a mortgage were after a certain period of time, the interest rate adjust. This adjustment is usually upwards, and is usually a large adjustment. The way lenders entice home buyers to take a loan of this nature, knowing that the fixed product with a fixed interest rate exist, is by offering it with lower initial interest rates and closing cost.

Although this type of loan seems dangerous, it does has its perks, and in some cases is the best option for someone buying a home and looking for a quality mortgage. A person that should want an ARM is someone that doesn't expect to be in the home long, and plans to sell within a set period of time, say 3, 5, or 7 years.

The interest rate tied to an ARM is usually fixed for a certain period of time, and then adjust, generally in accordance to an index, such as the LIBOR or MTA. Although the ARM is amortized over a 30 year period, if you plan on being in a home for the long term, say at least 10, 20 years, I recommend staying away from adjustable rate mortgages as it can increase your payment almost double in some scenarios depending on the position of the index when the mortgage adjust.

The popularity of each ARM is hard to determine because it all depends on the specific needs and intentions of the borrower. For example, if I was planning on staying in a home for four to five years, I would consider a five year ARM, because it gives me a fixed interest rate for the entire time period that I plan on keeping the home.

A few ARM products, listed in order of length are the 3/1 ARM, 5/1 ARM, and 7/1 ARM. The first number in the equation represents the number of years it is fixed for, and the 1 at the end of the equation represents how often it can adjust. For example a 5/1 ARM has a fixed interest rate for the first five years, and can adjust every one year after that.

3/1 ARM

A 3/1 ARM is a popular product for someone who expects to be in a home for three or less years. The interest rate on the 3/1 ARM is generally less than all other mortgage products as it only give the borrower a three year time frame of security where the interest rate is fixed before it adjust.

The closing cost of a three year loan are also generally less than most other mortgage products for the same reason as stated above. Anytime a person thinks they'll be in the home for longer than 3 years, I wouldn't recommend a 3 year ARM.

5/1 ARM

The 5/1 ARM is very similar to the 3/1 ARM as it is fixed for a certain period of time before it adjust. It has a slightly higher interest rate than a 3/1 ARM, as well as slightly higher closing cost since it gives two more years of security for the borrower.

The more security you want from your mortgage the more you will have to pay for it.

Interest Only Mortgages

An interest only mortgage provides a borrower with a lower monthly payment than that of a traditional mortgage that pays principle and interest. An interest only mortgage is generally amortized over 30 years, but for a certain period of time, only interest payments are required.

For example, a 30 year fixed, with a 10 year interest only option, would have a fixed interest rate for the entire 30 years, but only interest payments are due in the first ten years. For the remaining 20 years of the mortgage, it would then basically turn into a 20 year fixed as the entire principle balance would then be amortized over the remaining 20 years of the loan.

Over the last few years this product has become extremely popular in places like California, and South Florida where property values have risen to unaffordable levels. This is just another example of the mortgage industry's attempt to give everyone a chance at homeownership.

Interest only loans generally have a higher interest rate and higher closing cost than a traditional principle and interest loan, as the lender assumes more risk since the borrower isn't paying back any principle for a fixed period of time while the mortgage is in the interest only stage.

Balloon Mortgage

A balloon mortgage is one that can be very dangerous if not used correctly. A balloon mortgage is generally fixed for a certain period of time, and when that fixed period is up, the remaining balance is due in full.

For example, a 15 year balloon would be amortized over 30 years still, but you would only make payments on it for 15 years. After the 15 year period was over with, the remaining balance of the mortgage would then be due in full at that point.

For this reason, a person looking to stay in a home for a long time shouldn't generally use a balloon mortgage to achieve their mortgage goals as they can end up with a large mortgage payment after the balloon period is over.

In the case of a 15 year (180 months) balloon, the remaining balance would be due month 181. So instead of paying the regular $1200 monthly payment that you've been paying for the last 15 years, your payment that month could be $98,000 or whatever the remaining balance is at that time.

Generally, balloon mortgages are only given on second mortgages as part of an 80/20 loan (when two loans are given instead of one for 100% financing to avoid private mortgage insurance), but may be given on first mortgages as well depending on the lender.

This product can definitely catch a family off guard, especially if they forgot about the balloon payment, or it wasn't described to them properly by the mortgage lender who sold them the product.

The benefits of a balloon mortgage, is that the interest rates are generally less than other mortgage types, and the closing cost are usually much less as well. This is because the lender expects to get their money back in 15 years when the balloon payment is due.

If a person expects to sell the home before the balloon period occurs, than this may be a good product for them and their family. Other than that, it is a very scary thought getting your mortgage bill and seeing that your monthly payment has increased from $1200 a month to all of a sudden a $98,000 payment is due.

Pay Option ARM

A pay option arm is another product that can be very scary, especially if the loan officer who sold it to you didn't know much about the product himself. Often this product is referred to as a negative amortization loan, as if used in a certain way, the mortgage balance that you owe gets bigger and bigger every month, instead of smaller and smaller like most conventional and traditional mortgages.

The pay option ARM gives the borrower 3 options of what payment they want to pay each month when they receive their bill. Depending on the payment that the borrower decides to pay can determine if the mortgage balance gets smaller, stays the same or get larger.

In regards to the pay option ARM, the three choices that are available for the borrower is the principle and interest payment, interest only payment, and a partial interest payment.

With the first option, which is paying the principle and interest payment, the balance of the mortgage would actually get smaller, but this option is hardly ever chosen by someone that has taken a pay option ARM, as they took the mortgage because they couldn't afford the regular monthly payment.

With the second option, which is paying the interest only payment, the balance of the mortgage would stay the same as no principle was paid and all of the interest was paid.

The last option is generally the one chosen by most borrowers who decide to get a pay option ARM, which is to only pay a portion of the interest charged for that month. This is very dangerous as the remaining interest that went unpaid is added to the principle of the mortgage, thus making your mortgage balance larger each month that you decide to make this payment.

This is even scarier when used on a home that is in an area where the property values are decreasing, as opposed to growing in value. In this scenario, the amount owed the bank would continue to grow month after month, while the value of the home would continue to decrease from month to month.

This could put someone in a very tough situation as they can end up owing more for the home than it is worth, which is considered being "up-side down" in the mortgage industry.

I would only okay this product for affluent individuals who have a very good understanding of this product and have a very strong financial situation that would allow them to handle an "upside down" situation, if one was to ever occur, which is very likely if the borrower is continuously only making the minimum monthly payments, and the remaining interest is added to the principle balance each month.

Of all the mortgage products available, I hope that I have made it clear that the one that is best for you depend upon your particular needs and intentions for the home, including how long you plan on living in or ultimately owning the property.

Closing Cost

Closing cost are charged for practically every mortgage loan. Even though some lenders will deceive you and tell you that they aren't charging you any closing cost for the loan, they are generally just hidden.

What I mean by hidden is that if they are not charged to you up front at closing, they will generally be charged to you by way of a higher interest rate, or with pre-payment penalties (large fee for paying off the mortgage early).

Closing cost are fees associated with the lender providing you with the loan. They sometimes break the fee down into countless items, which I think is more confusing than anything, and some will just charge you one upfront fee for the loan.

When companies decide to break these fees down, they generally list them as origination, processing, underwriting, discount points (if any), application fee, and several other "junk fees". I don't like this idea, as what matters to me is the total fee that the lender is charging me for the loan.

I have no care (and you shouldn't either) to know exactly what depart-ment my money is going to, because once it's in the lenders hands, it can't be any benefit to me, thus giving me no reason to care about how the company is going to be dividing the money.

What matters to me is the total fee that I'm paying for the loan to the lender. This is very similar to how Mc. Donald's and many other regular businesses operate. They don't give a break down of how the cost of the Big Mac added up to $2.39. Even if they did offer a break down, there's no reason to want it as the only thing that should matter is the total cost that you are paying for the sandwich.

On top of the fees that the lender charges for the loan, other closing cost would include what is called "third parties" such as appraisal, title insurance, and closing attorney fee. These fees usually add up to about $1,500 to $2,500 depending on the size and value of the house.

In some states there are also government and transfer taxes that must be paid at closing, but similar to the third party fees, these are not charges from the lender and will have to be paid no matter what lender you use.

Because closing cost also include third party fees, when the lender fees are broken into 15 different fees, they can be confused as third parties and vice versa. A good way to measure the total lender fees that you are paying from one lender to the next for a loan is to compare the APR's for the same interest rate.

The APR for a mortgage is described as the total cost of the loan put into an annual percentage rate. What this means is that it takes the interest rate and adds in the closing cost to come up with a percentage rate that you are actually paying for the loan over the entire duration of the loan.

This is a good way to compare one lender to another. For example, if both companies are offering a 30 year fixed with an interest rate of 6.25%, but the APR for one of the companies is 6.5% vs. 6.78 for the other, this would let you know that the company with the higher APR is the one that is charging you the most in lender fees, which is what's important, as your third party closing cost and taxes are going to be the same with any lender that you use even if they tell you different.

In an attempt to make you think that they have the lower fees, some lenders will sometimes give low ball estimates on your third party closing cost to make your total closing cost look less than they really are. This is very deceitful, and the way to overcome falling victim to this, is to compare the APR between each mortgage company that you are considering doing business with.

Private Mortgage Insurance

Private mortgage insurance, also know as "PMI" is required for all prime mortgages that don't have at least 20% down. The borrower pays for the policy that covers the lender in case the borrower defaults on the loan.

Generally, the borrower gets no benefit from paying private mortgage insurance as the lender is the only one who benefits from it in case the borrower defaults on the loan and the lender is forced to foreclose and sell the property to try and get their money back.

Where the lender benefits from the private mortgage insurance is that depending on the policy that they have, if they need to foreclose on the property and sell it, the difference from what they sell the home for and the remaining balance left on the mortgage is made up by the insurance company that underwrote the private mortgage insurance policy.

Once the loan to value is 80% or less, the borrower no longer has to pay private mortgage insurance and it falls off of the monthly payment. There are generally two ways to get the PMI taken off: If the mortgage balance goes down to 80% of the original home value at the time of purchase, then the lender will automatically drop the PMI from your monthly payment as they are required to do so by law.

The second way to get PMI off of your monthly payment is if your home appreciates in value, so that you now have 20% of equity in the home. If this is the case, you must call the lender and pay them to have a licensed appraiser come out and appraise the home. If they find out that the home has appreciated to a point where it gives you 20% equity, then they will promptly remove the PMI from your mortgage payment.

PMI is very undesirable as it has no benefit to the borrower and is not even tax deductible. A way to get 100% financing without having to pay PMI is to get an 80/20 "Piggy Back" loan. With an 80/20 loan, you get two separate loans, one for 80% of the mortgage and another for the remaining 20% of the mortgage.

The second mortgage that's for the smaller amount generally has a much higher interest rate than the first mortgage as it is more risk on the second loan as it is sometimes with a totally different lender than the first mortgage.

Even though the interest rate on the second mortgage is generally a lot higher than that of the first, the monthly payment generally still comes out cheaper than doing the one loan that has PMI.

Another benefit of doing an 80/20 loan is that instead of paying PMI, with the piggyback, the extra interest paid on the high interest rate on the second mortgage is tax deductible, while no portion of the PMI payment is deductible.

Pre-Payment Penalties

Pre-payment penalties are generally only placed on sub prime loans, but in some cases a prime lender will try and sneak in a pre-payment penalty on the loan in order to make more profit on the loan, especially if it's a broker or a lender that sells off their mortgages in the secondary market.

If a loan has a pre-payment penalty tied to it, the borrower will be penalized if they sell the home, refinance, or pay off the mortgage early during the pre payment penalty phase. The pre payment penalty usually ranges from 1 to 5% of the original mortgage amount, which could really add up if the loan if big enough.

When it comes to pre payment penalties, there are "hard" and "soft" penalties. A hard penalty will penalize you if you make any additional payments to principle during the pre-payment penalty phase, where as a soft penalty only penalizes the borrower if they pay off the entire mortgage during the pre-payment penalty phase.

Pre-payment penalties are very unattractive, as they attempt to lock a borrower into a loan, potentially longer than they want to be in the loan, especially if the home appreciates rapidly and they have profitable offers to sell their home. With a pre-payment penalty on a loan, it can really take away a lot of options that would normally be good choices if no pre-payment penalty existed.

If you have a good credit history, do not accept a pre payment penalty on your mortgage as there are many lenders that will give you a loan without a pre-payment penalty. When working with a mortgage broker, it is of the essence to make sure they don't add a pre-payment penalty to your loan, as they will often do so to make an additional profit.

The only prime loan that commonly comes with a pre-payment penalty is the pay option ARM. With a 3 year pre payment penalty, on a $500,000 loan, the broker's profit would be $15,000. Generally, with the pay option ARM, each year of pre-payment penalty that is added to a loan gives the broker 1% of profit based on the loan amount.

So do all you can to stay away from pre-payment penalties as they will hinder you from making many important decisions that would normally be easy to make if there wasn't any pre-payment penalty involved.

Also, if you have great credit there are many lenders out there that will give you a great loan without any prepayment penalties, and if a lender is trying to pass one on to you, it may be wise to find someone else to finance your home purchase, as a loan officer that does this to someone with good credit is likely to be unethical and possibly makes a living giving customers mortgages that are not in their best interest.

Refinancing

Refinancing a mortgage means getting a new loan on a home that you already own and have a mortgage on, or at some point had a mortgage on if it has been paid off. There are two main reasons for a person to refinance a loan: Rate and Term, and to get cash out.

Rate and Term Refinance

There are generally two situations, when a person would do a rate and term refinance. The first reason is if they have an adjustable rate mortgage that has adjusted or is about to adjust and the borrower wants to lock in a lower fixed interest rate for the remainder of the loan.

The second reason for someone to do a rate and term refinance is if they locked in an interest rate when rates where relatively high, and interest rates have come down to where refinancing is a great option, in order to lock in a lower payment.

Cash out Refinancing

There's generally only one reason to do a cash out refinance, and that is to get some cash out. The reasons why you may want to get the cash out are plenty, and may include doing some home improvements, to bail your husband or wife out of jail (women go to jail too), or to pay off some credit cards.

Generally when doing a cash out refinance, a lender will allow a borrower to raise the loan amount to 95% of the value of the home in cash.

When doing a refinance, both rate and term and cash out, it's important to know that you have a 3 day rescission period after closing and signing all the paperwork to cancel and back out of the loan. The 3 day period includes Saturdays, but not Sundays and holidays.

If for any reason after closing on a refinance you feel uncomfortable with the new loan that you've selected, you can back out within 3 days with no penalty.

Summary of Chapter

Knowing the basics of any business will allow you to operate within that world, and the least give you what you need to be able to oversee a transaction to know what's going on and if someone is getting played or not, which is very important as it may be you that's the one getting played.

Mortgage information is also very valuable as you will need one to invest in the best investment in the world: Real estate, and it's good to know your mortgage options as picking the right mortgage for you, might determine if the investment you made is going to be profitable. For more mortgage info, visit www.BlackBusinessSmart.blogspot.com.

CHAPTER 5
WHAT YOU NEED TO KNOW ABOUT INVESTING IN STOCKS

Growing up as a young boy, and then later on as a teenager, I would watch the news with my mom and wonder to my self "Who is this Dow Jones guy they keep talking about everyday on the 5:00 news"? I figured he had to be pretty important, but when I asked my mom who he was, I found out that she didn't have the slightest clue.

I later found out that the Dow Jones guy actually wasn't a person, but if it was a person he would definitely be important. In the stock market, the Dow Jones Industrial Average is a collection of 30 of the largest companies in the country, and it measures their performance collectively as a whole on a day to day basis (Monday-Friday).

Throughout this chapter, we will definitely be going into depth on all I feel you need to know about investing in stocks, and by the end of this chapter, you will know just as well as I do, who "Dow Jones" is.

Although stocks may have looked bad in my comparison to real estate, stocks can be a very good investment if used with the right game plan. One last time for the record, I do say that real estate is my favorite investment (and should be yours also), but stocks have made many investors very wealthy, and can be a great piece to any sound investment puzzle.

I do not however believe that a person's investments should be in all stocks, just as I don't believe a person's dinner should be made up of all side orders. A person wouldn't go to Kentucky Fried Chicken or Popeye's and order one macaroni, one mashed potato, one green been, and one order of fries.

On the other hand, a person could go to one of those restaurants and order just chicken, which is the main dish. In my comparison, I'm comparing real estate to chicken, and stocks to side orders. You can have a main dish without any sides, but rarely will person order sides, without any main dish.

Like I mentioned earlier, stocks can be a great investment if used properly, and through out this chapter, I will be teaching you how to use them properly to maximize profits, while minimizing the potential for losses at the same time.

I will be sharing with you a lot of things that you may have never heard of, so I expect that by the end of this chapter, you can compare what you've learned to when you where a kid and first learned to read. Now you probably couldn't imagine not being able to read, and such will be the same when finished with this chapter. It will be like you were blind; but now you can see....

Stocks.....What Are They?

I guess before we discuss who Dow Jones is, I should tell you what a stock is....But I decided I'm not going to. That's right, I'm not too happy with my stock portfolio right now, and so I'm not going to teach you what a stock is. What are you going to do? Sue me? The rest of this book will be filled with my baby pictures as I will take you through my life as an infant all the way to adult hood.....(Just joking)

A stock, which is also used interchangeably with the word "share", represents ownership of a business. So it can be said that if you are a shareholder of a particular company, say General Motors or Nike for instance, then you are a part owner of that company. Stocks can be divided between common stock and preferred stock. 99% of the time when investing in stocks it will be in common stocks. Not all companies issue preferred stock, although is does provide a shareholder with certain distinct benefits.

Owners of preferred stock get paid dividends before those of common stock, and if the company went bankrupt, they would get money before owners of common stock. On the downside, only owners of common stock can vote on issues of management, and acquiring or merging with other companies.

Generally, only small amounts of preferred stock is normally issued, as "common" stock is what's most common as it gives you real ownership powers such as voting on mergers, or who should be on the board of directors.

When a business decides to incorporate (will be discussed in a later chapter) their business into a C-Corporation, the company gets authorized to issue a certain number of shares, which is equivalent to selling pieces of ownership in the business.

Shares of a business can be compared to cutting a pie into many pieces. The more pieces of the pie you own, the more of the company you own also. Incorporating a business and issuing (selling) shares is just like dividing the ownership of a business into many pieces, and whoever holds the most pieces individually or collectively, has the most control over the company.

Just like any other business, the shareholders of most major companies get their fair share of profits when they are distributed by way of dividends (will be covered later in this chapter).

Being a shareholder definitely has its privileges besides sharing in profit, as the more of the company that you own, the more control you have over that company. Shareholders are responsible for voting for the board of directors, who in return oversee the company and hire for top company positions such as president and chief executive officer.

Shareholders have the right to attend shareholder annual meetings, where they can participate in voting on company issues such as if the company should acquire another company, or even if it should merge and become partners with another.

This means that if a person is able to get a large enough share of the company, they could heavily influence the direction of the company and maybe even place themselves into an executive position, but that all depends on if you own a large enough piece of the pie to vote yourself in.

Most large companies that we buy our everyday products from, such as Wal-Mart, Home Depot, Mc. Donald's, Reebok, and Target are considered "public" companies, and have shares that are available for purchase by the general public.

This gives any and everybody, from the president of the United States, to the janitor in charge of changing light bulbs at the local hospital, a chance to own a piece of the largest companies of the world. Each company has its own ticker symbol that's used when buying and selling stocks on the stock market. For example, General Motors' ticker symbol is "GM", and Wal-Mart's ticker symbol is "wmt"

Classification of Stocks

Stocks are often classified based on the type of company it is, the company's value, or in some cases the level of return that is expected from the company. Some companies grow faster than others, while some have reached what they perceive as their peak and don't think they can handle more growth. In some cases, management just might be content with the level of business that they've achieved, thus stalling to make moves to gain further business.

Before investing in a particular company, it is very important to get to know the company on a personal level and find out what the company's goals and objectives are for the short and long term. Some company's are growth minded, while some are defensive minded and operate in services that are always needed such as food.

In order to prosper in the world of stock investing, a person must have a clear understanding of what they are doing, or they shouldn't be doing it at all. Stocks can be a very risky investment, depending on the level of knowledge held by the person(s) making the investment decisions. So learn all you can, and as I quoted Rev Run in the real estate chapter, "choose wisely". Below is a list of classifications that I find important to know.

Blue Chip Stocks

Blue chip stocks represent the largest companies in the world such as Wal-Mart, American Express, General Motors, and Home Depot. These companies usually have very high earnings year after year, and have a reputation of stability and exceptional corporate management.

These companies have great financial strength, and often share the profits of the business on a quarterly basis. These companies aren't as concerned with growth, because due to their business model, the more people that are born, creates automatic business for a lot of these companies.

Because of the financial strength of most blue chips, they generally make for good investments year around, as long as the company that you are investing in, shares your personal goals and objectives. If you are looking to invest in a company that will grow at a rapid pace, and a company tells you that they are maintaining their current size as they can't handle more business right now, then this is not the company for you as they don't share your current objectives.

And for you information, in case you have any doubt, yes, the Dow Jones Industrial Average that I spoke of earlier in the chapter is composed of 30 blue chip companies.

Growth Stocks

Growth stocks represent companies whose sales and profits are growing faster then the rest of the economy or their individual sector for that matter. These companies are usually very aggressive and are actively acquiring other companies to help them achieve their growth goals.

These companies usually have a very aggressive marketing plan, and focus heavily on branding their name, which ultimately gets their product inside of our homes. These companies may be blue chips at the same time, if they are unhappy with their position and have turned growth minded, but usually growth stocks are of companies that have yet made a strong dominating mark in their industry.

Growth stocks usually don't pay dividends (share profits) to shareholders during the growth stages of the company, as they retain the majority of company profits, as they are used to grow the company with, which can often mean acquiring (buying) other companies.

So as I said before, if you are considering investing in stocks, get to know the company on a personal level before you invest in it, because their company goals may be the exact opposite of your personal investment goals. If you are looking for a company that will pay you dividends (company profits) every quarter, then a growth stock is not what you are looking for.

Defensive Stocks

Defensive stocks are companies that are generally stable all year around as they are companies that provide important goods and services that are used in good as well as bad economic times. These would include shares of such businesses as electric companies, food suppliers, tobacco companies, and soda companies like Coca Cola and General Electric.

These companies will usually hold their own (market position) in the worst of economic times, such as a downturn or recession, thus making good investments during business cycles where other investments are plunging, or declining rapidly in value.

Income Stocks

Income stocks are generally some of my favorite stocks as they offer above average dividend (profit) payments to their shareholders. These companies are usually very stable, and have gained a large market share, as they can afford to heavily reward their shareholders.

Income stocks are usually very attractive to retired people that depend on the consistent dividend payments every quarter. These are companies that are usually comfortable and content with their current market position and have focused on maintaining their current business, versus trying to gain new business. This is not always the case but generally it is.

Cyclical Stocks

Cyclical stocks are stocks of companies whose sales and profits generally fluctuate (move up & down) depending on the business cycle or condition of the economy. For example, during bad economic times, cyclical stock prices decline and in good economic times their earnings and stock price increase.

Although cyclical stocks can be used to maximize profits in recovering and expanding economic times, I'm not a fan of high volatility. In times of prolonging economic hardship, these company's stock prices generally continue to decrease and sometimes these company's fall into bankruptcy and loose their market position all together.

Large Cap Stocks

Large cap stocks are generally blue ship companies that are powerhouse businesses and have a large piece of the market share. This is not always the case however, as some large cap companies have negative earnings (losses instead of profits) and declining sales.

This is possible because, unlike blue chip companies that get their name from being stable and proven companies, a large cap company is just a company with market capitalization of over $10 billion. The market capitalization of a company is determined by multiplying the company's stock price by the number of shares outstanding (shares issued to the public).

During the period right before the stock bubble burst is a good example of when many companies didn't even have revenues, but because of an inflated stock price were labeled as large cap companies. Of course you got to earn the title of being a blue chip company with long term sales and profits.

Mid Cap Stocks

A mid cap company is a company with a market capitalization of greater than $2 billion, but less the $10 billion. These companies are usually growth companies that are on their way to being large cap, and hopefully blue chip companies.

A mid cap stock may be a good investment depending on your investment goals, as a mid cap stock can possibly be a growth or income company depending on their business philosophy.

Generally a mid cap company will not pay any dividends as they are using all of the company's profits to grow and expand their current level of business. This is usually okay with their share holders as they invested for growth and not for dividends, unless they invested without knowing what they invested in.

Small Cap Stocks

Small cap stocks are stocks of companies that have less than $2 billion in market capitalization. These are usually growth companies with very aggressive marketing plans, as they're in a position to either sink or swim.

Small cap companies rarely ever pay any dividends, as they generally need every dollar that they can get to help either expand the business, or in many scenarios to stay afloat. Many small cap companies go out of business before making it out of the small cap category, which makes this a very critical stage in the life of the business.

No matter what your goals are, it is very important to know exactly what business cycle you are in, as well as the detailed business profile of the company that you are considering investing in. It is very important to know exactly what you are doing before you start doing it.

Mutual Funds

With all the talk of the need for diversification in today's marketplace, a lot of people are turning to mutual funds. A mutual fund is a collection of companies from different sectors, industries, market caps, and often countries that make up one share.

If a person buys one share of a mutual fund, they would potentially own a piece of approximately 100 companies. To some people this is considered diversification as they own a piece of many companies instead of just one or a few.

For the record, I believe diversification is being in several totally different investments. For example, owning two hotels, a book publishing company, a clothing line, and shares of Coca Cola and Exxon Mobil would symbolize diversification to me. It doesn't have to be in these specifics businesses or stocks, but hopefully you get the picture.

In regards to having a diversified portfolio, my opinion on mutual funds is that they are for amateur investors who don't know how to pick their own investments, or for one reason or another don't have time to. From the ages of 18 to 20, before I had a good understanding of investing, I depended upon mutual funds myself for diversification or at least for what my perception of diversification was at the time.

Although mutual funds can give a person professional management of investments, the downside to that is mutual fund companies generally charge large fees that eat a large portion of the profits on a continual basis. I'm not at all a fan of this, especially when the mutual fund company doesn't assume any of the risk.

On the upside, there are mutual funds that are tied to indexes such as the S&P 500 (measure of the stock performance of 500 of the largest companies) that have much smaller fees than traditional mutual funds as less work and research is performed since they are just tied to the index.

Depending on the investment skill level of an individual, mutual funds may need to play a vital role in a person's investment portfolio in order to give them some level of diversification that they would normally not otherwise have if making all investment decisions on their own.

After I learned more about investing, particularly in real estate, I took out all of my money that I had in mutual funds and bought a duplex, and then another home six months later.

Exchange Markets

Just like the farmers in the first chapter, stock investors need a place to trade and exchange their stocks and thus exchange markets exist. There are many exchange markets, but only two exist that I feel the need to cover.

The exchange markets that I'm going to cover in order of popularity are the New York Stock Exchange (NYSE) and NASDAQ.

New York Stock Exchange

The New York Stock Exchange (NYSE) was created in 1792 and is the largest exchange for stocks (equities) in the world. It is commonly referred to as the Big Board as it is the home to a majority of the largest companies in the world.

A stock can only be traded on one exchange, and elite companies such as Wal-Mart, Exxon Mobil, Home Depot, and General Motors have all decided to have their shares traded on the New York Stock Exchange. It is very likely that if investing in stocks, the company you have bought a piece of ownership in, will be listed as a member of the New York Stock Exchange.

Currently there are approximately 1400 members (companies) of the New York Stock Exchange, and they all pay a pretty penny to have their company listed and exchanged. In addition to that nice ransom, all members of the NYSE have to meet strict requirements relating to the value of the stock, average trading volume, number of shareholders, and company earnings.

The majority of all companies listed on the NYSE are stable businesses, and the ones who loose their stability generally get de-listed or kicked off of the exchange. Stocks begin trading on the NYSE at 9:30 am eastern time and close at 4:00 pm. The NYSE is open Monday through Friday, and is closed for most recognized holidays.

NASDAQ

Behind the NYSE, I consider NASDAQ as the most prestigious exchange in North America, and possibly in the world. Although it may have sounded like every big company is a member of the NYSE, there are several very high profile companies that are listed on the NASDAQ.

The NASDAQ is highly regarded as the exchange for Tech stocks, and is home to big names such as Microsoft, YAHOO!, Intel, Cisco, and Apple Computers. Similar to the NYSE, there is also very strict criteria that must be met in order to be listed on the NASDAQ and therefore most companies listed there are quality companies in terms of having a certain level of sales and assets.

During the "tech boom" in the late 90's and early 2000, it was mostly companies that were traded on the NASDAQ that became extremely overpriced and was the reason behind the infamous "bubble burst". A lot of these companies had stock prices that were rapidly appreciating, but the companies weren't making any profits. This definitely caught up to investors as the true value eventually came to life on many of these companies, and in some instances the true value that was discovered was $0.

Types of Orders

Before making any investment decisions involving stocks, it is essential to know what type of orders can be made and how to read certain pertinent information that will be displayed to you when researching various companies' stock information.

First and foremost it is important to know and understand some basic yet important terminology. When receiving a stock quote, there are generally three important things that you should want to know right away. The first is the current value of the stock. This is established as the last price that the stock was sold for. When you hear that a stock is trading at $25 per share, that means that the last trade of the stock between a buyer and a seller was for $25.

The next two important things that you should know and understand is the "bid" and "ask" price. The bid price represents the highest price that someone is willing to pay for the stock at any given moment, and the ask price represents the lowest price that a seller is willing to sell the stock for.

Something very important to note is anytime the bid price is higher than the current value or "last" price, than someone is willing to pay more than the stock is currently worth, which will raise the value of the stock to the latest purchase price, if indeed the person bidding was successful in buying shares.

Also if the bid price is far below the current value or "last" price, that means that the market is not in high demand of that particular company's stock and if the stock is sold below current market value, than the stock price will decrease with it, as the value or stock price only represents the last price that the stock was sold for.

On the flipside though, if the bid price is far above the current market value and the ask is above also, and the two meet somewhere above current market value, then the stock price will increase accordingly to what the last stock sold for.

When placing orders to purchase stock, there are many options that a person can make in deciding what type of order to make, and I'll be discussing the ones that I feel are important for you to know.

Market Order

A market order is the most common type of order in the market place. A market order doesn't request that the stocks be bought or sold at a certain price. It just asked that the transaction takes place at whatever the going rate is in the market place.

When someone makes a market order request, they are not concerned with buying or selling at a certain price and are generally comfortable with whatever the going rate is at the time of the request. For example, if someone makes a market request to buy some of General Motor's stock, and the going price is $29, then that is the price that they are going to pay.

Buy Limit Order

A buy limit order is an order that request that the designated stock be purchased at a certain price or below. For example, if Wal-Mart stock is trading at $49, and an investor wants some, but doesn't think its worth more than $47, thus not wanting to pay more than $47 for it, he can put in a buy limit order of $47. When the stock price dip down to $47 or below, the stock will be purchased for the going price, as long as it is less than $47.

A buy limit order is a very good way to protect yourself from paying more than a certain price for a stock, especially if you've noticed a high level of volatility in the price of the stock and want to capitalize and buy it.

For example, if you noticed that Exxon Mobil's stock price constantly fluctuates from $65 to $67 on a daily basis, and you wanted to buy some at the low point, then a buy limit order at $65 would buy the stock for you when it was again available at $65.

Sell Limit Order

A sell limit order is very similar to a buy limit order, but in this case as the name indicates, it involves selling a stock instead of buying one. A sell limit order is a request to sell a currently owned stock at or above a certain price. This sell limit price is usually higher than the current market price.

For example, lets use help from the example above, and say that after buying the Exxon Mobil stock for $65, your wanted to sell it as soon as the price went back up to $67, as you noticed it's been doing for the last couple of weeks in your observations. In this case you would place a sell limit order of $67, and as soon as the going rate was $67 again, your stock would be sold, thus making you a quick profit.

A sell limit order is a good way to sell a stock at a certain price without having to watch the market and waiting until the market was paying a certain amount for the stock. With a sell limit order, you can just place it, and whenever the stock price goes back up, your shares would automatically sell.

Options Trading Basics

Options can be very risky if used the wrong way. They can also be very rewarding if used correctly, similar to any investment, but it is much more serious with options as you could potentially loose more money than you can dream of.

Options are a very good investment if you are the one buying them, and potentially suicide if you are the one selling them. For the record, unless you are filthy rich, do not sell any options (you'll see why shortly) that require you to buy or sell a stock at a certain price, especially if it's not covered.

On the positive side, purchasing the right kind of option can be like having insurance on your stock in case the price declines. Also, a certain option can be purchased on a stock that you don't own, and if the stock price rapidly increase, your option gives you the right to buy the stock at the low price that's agreed to on your option.

Let's take a look at some of the option choices out there, and which ones to stay away from. If you go against what I'm about tell you, you may need more than this book to gain wealth, as you may end up in a whole that is way too deep to climb out of.

Call Options

A call option can be your best friend, but if used the wrong way, it can quickly turn into the greatest enemy that you ever had. A call option gives the owner of it the right to purchase (call) a specific stock at a certain price (strike price), no matter what the real value of it is.

For example, if I own a call option on Nike stock with a strike price of $30, and the stock rises to $100, the person who sold me the call would be forced to sell me the stock for $30, even though it is now worth $100 per share. Obviously this would give me a quick $70 per share profit, without having much initial risk, as I only paid pennies on the dollar for the option to buy, instead of buying the stock outright.

On the other hand, the person who sold me the call option would be in a deep world of mess. If he owned enough shares of the stock to satisfy my order than he could just give me his shares, but if not, then he would have to buy the shares at the current market price of $100 per share, and then turn around and sell them to me for only $30 (my strike price) per share.

This could obviously put him in a horrible situation, and one that I don't ever want any of my readers to be in, because it could turn out much worse than this. What if the stock price went up to $2,000 a share? The person who sold me the option would have to go out and buy enough shares to satisfy my request at the market price of $2,000 per share and then sell them to me at $30 (my strike price) and loose a ton of money in the process.

If the person was covered (owned the shares that he sold me the option on), then instead of being forced to buy the shares at market price, he would loose out on what could've been a magnificent profit, since he would have to sell me his shares at only $30, instead of being able to sell them at the current market price of $2,000 a share.

Like I said, a call option could be your best friend if used properly, so it is important that you understand how to use one. For example, let's imagine that you've been watching a certain company's stock and you believe it is getting ready for a strong upturn, but you're not sure.

Instead of buying 1,000 shares of the company's stock, which would be an expensive investment and a potential large risk, you could buy 10 options (each option gives you the option to purchase 100 shares) that would that would give you the right to buy 1,000 shares at a specified price, so you can still profit from the stock's price gain (if it actually does increases) without having to actually own the shares at the time of the increase.

Put Option

Similar to a call option, if purchased, a put option could also be your best friend, and used like an insurance policy for a stock that you currently own to protect yourself against a downturn. A put option gives the owner of a stock the right to sell (put) a stock to the seller of the put option at a specified price, no matter of what the actual stock price is. For example, let's say I buy 100 shares of Wal-Mart stock at $50 per share. If for some reason the stock price declined to $0, I would be at a loss of $5,000, unless I bought some "insurance" (a put option).

If in this scenario, I purchased a put option with a strike price (right to sell price) of $50 immediately after I bought the stock, and then the stock price declined to $0, I would still be able to sell my shares to the seller of the put option for $50 per share, thus my only loss would be the price I paid for the "insurance" (put option).

In this scenario the seller of the put option would be the one out of $5,000, minus the small revenue he received from selling me the put option, which would probably only be around $500, thus giving him a net loss of $4500, and giving me a loss of only $500. This is good for me as I could've been at a loss of $5,000 instead of just $500.

As you can tell, buying a put option for protection is a great idea, while selling a put option to someone else can be a natural disaster waiting to happen. The thought of being forced to buy a stock for $50 that's no longer worth anything should show you the seriousness and potential dangers of selling put options.

Like with any investment, options can be good or bad depending on the level of knowledge of the investor. Also, one last note for selling call options, they are particularly extra risky because there's no limit to how high a stock price can go, thus giving the seller of the call an infinite amount of risk.

There are a lot more option choices and strategies available, but they are very advanced and not necessary for this book, as the basics will do you just fine.

Fundamental Analysis

When investing in stocks, choosing wisely can be just as important as it is with purchasing real estate. Knowing when a stock is under priced or over priced for that matter can be a very powerful skill that can make or save an investor a ton of money.

There are certain tools that will be explained in this section that can be used in what is considered "fundamental analysis". Fundamental analysis doesn't focus on the economy as much as it does the financial condition of a company and its' stock price.

The following set of ratios are used in fundamental analysis, to examine the condition of a company and its' stock price to help an investor make a wise investment decision.

Earnings Per Share (EPS)

The Earnings per share of a company is closely watched by Wall Street and is used to determine if a company met its' earnings goal and Wall Street expectations. A company's earnings per share (EPS) is calculated by subtracting money paid out for preferred dividends from the net income, and then divided by the number of shares outstanding (owned by the public).

For easy math sake, let's say that Nike had a quarterly profit of $10,500, and paid out $500 in preferred dividends. That would then leave $10,000 to be divided by the number of shares that are outstanding. Let's say that Nike only had 1,000 shares outstanding. That would then give them an earnings per share of $1.00 ($10,000/1,000 =$1.00)

Often when a company's earnings are released on a quarterly basis, the first thing that is calculated is the company's earnings per share. Generally if a company missed its goal, or came short of Wall Street's expectations, the stock price will fall. On the other hand, if a company's earnings come back stronger than expected, the stock price will generally increase. When earnings are equal to goals and expectations, the stock price usually isn't affected as stocks constantly adjust based on what is expected of company's earnings in the future.

Price to Earnings Ratio

The price to earnings ratio of a company is also very heavily watched by Wall Street, but can't be calculated until after a company's earnings per share ratio has been calculated. A company's price to earnings (P/E) ratio is often used to measure if a company is trading for more than it is worth based on earnings.

A company's price to earnings ratio is calculated by dividing the current market price of a stock by it's earnings per share. For example, let's say that Nike was currently trading at $30 and had earnings per share of $1.00 (based on example above for EPS). To find the company's price to earnings ratio (P/E) you would divide the $30 share price by the $1.00 earnings per share and come up with a price to earnings ratio of 30 ($30/$1.00 = 30).

It has been said that a price to earnings ratio under 32 is very good, and generally represents an under priced (value) stock. This is not always the case as sometimes you do get what you pay for, so it is wise to get to know any company you decide to invest in on a personal level.

In some cases a company's stock price might be low due to talks of bankruptcy or a possible government investigation on some of the company's practices. So just because a company has a high earnings per share, and a low price to earnings ratio, it doesn't mean that you should just automatically invest in that company. That would be quite stupid actually and an unwise business decision.

There are many other ratios out there, including some that would be better discussed in an accounting book. I do feel that some are more important than others, and even further that some are practically non important at all for the individual investor. A lot of these ratios are used by corporate executives to see they are getting all that they can out of certain investments, e.t.c.

As a reminder, in addition to using these two important tools of fundamental analysis, it is important to base your investment decisions on several factors including the business cycle you are in, the goals and objective of the company, as well as your individual investment goals. These fundamental tools are just there to help you along the way.

Times To Invest In Stocks

Besides the abundance of opportunity with investing in real estate, another reason why stocks are not my favorite investment is because they do not make wise investments all year around and through every business cycle. Certain phases of the business cycle are much better than others for stock investing, as some are just plan out horrible for investing in stocks.

Good Times To Invest In Stocks

The two scenarios that I find to be perfect for investing in stocks is at the trough (lowest point in the business cycle) and during certain parts of an economic expansion. The first scenario is during the lowest point in the business cycle, and that is because when you are at the bottom the only way you can go is up. Generally at this point in the cycle, all of the amateur investors have sold off all of their good investments for relatively low prices to astute investors who understand when to be greedy.

The second scenario is when the economy is going through a lengthy expansion with very low interest rates as well as little to no inflation. This is a perfect scenario as it usually indicates that the economy flourishing and stocks will generally be the benefit. Usually in most expansions, the demand for goods are so high that inflation gets out of control, thus leading to rising interest rates.

So if an expansion is present with both low inflation and low interest rates, it is usually a great time to invest in stocks as business profits will likely continue to increase and set new earnings records, which normally will increase a company's stock price.

Bad Times To Invest In Stocks

As I said not all times are good times to invest in stocks, and actually there are times that are horrible to invest in stocks. Generally during bad times to invest in stocks you will hear co-workers at places like Home Depot, Mc. Donald's, and Wal-Mart talk about the latest stock that they've just purchased. When you hear this, you know it's time to sell many of your stock holdings to the amateurs who are now entering.

Generally it is well known that amateur investors jump into the market at the end of the up climb as they think they'll receive the same profits that were received by the people (astute investors) who bought the stock in the trough when prices were at their lowest point. Now amateur investors are getting in at the stock's highest point, and once at the top, the only place to go is down.

When the economy is expanding (continually growing to new heights) and signs start arising that the peak in near and that a retraction is coming, it is usually a very bad time to invest in stocks. Generally during an expansion that is nearing its' peak, housing starts will begin to decline, and interest rates will start to climb up also.

Another sign that the peak is near is that the retail sales report will start reporting stagnate or declining growth. As stated earlier, retail sales contribute to 2/3rds or 66% of the Gross Domestic Product (GDP) which is the ultimate indicator of where the economy is. If the monthly retail sales report is negative two months in a row, you can be sure that the Gross Domestic Product (GDP) numbers will be negative for the quarter, and two consecutive quarters of negative GDP growth is an official recession. I'm not sure if this needs to be repeated, but this is a BAD time to invest.

Don't Even Think About It

The worst time to invest in a stock is when you receive an email or fax telling you that a company is getting ready to explode. This is often considered a "hot stock tip", which is a scam 99.9999% of the time. No good company that is in a position to explode will need to do mass "junk" advertising of their stock.

Generally when you receive one of these faxes or emails, it is from someone who is looking to inflate the stock price and then quickly sell their shares before it drops back down to its' true value, which is often $0.

Also, don't take investment advice from uneducated (investment wise) co workers and friends. They will often give you the same advice that they've received in their email or through the fax machine, and commonly without telling you where they got the information from. Generally these people want to do all that they can to make it appear that they are important and maybe have a big connection within a large corporation.

When it comes to buying stocks based on this information, do me, your family, and yourself a big favor and "DON'T EVEN THINK ABOUT IT"!

Dividends

As briefly described before, dividends are the portion of company profits that the board of directors decide to share with it owners (shareholders). When issued, dividends are usually paid on a quarterly basis. They are generally either based on a % of the stock price, or a predetermined dollar amount that will be paid for each share that you own.

Not all companies pay dividends as they need them (profits) for growing the company. Companies that usually pay dividends are income companies that are already very large in nature and can afford to share their profits with the owners instead of using them for growing the company.

Most companies that do not pay dividends are growth companies and small to mid cap businesses as they are all generally in the growing stage, and it is vital to use every dollar wisely or they may not survive.

Generally retired and older people invest in income stocks for the income as they are too old to work and need the steady stream of income. Many others also invest in income stocks as some stocks are a mix of growth and income stocks and provide an investor with steady income as well as an appreciating stock price.

Sometimes a company will decide to pay a dividend that normally doesn't. For example, in 2005 Microsoft, which is known as a non-dividend paying company decided to pay a multi billion dollar dividend to be divided between its' shareholders as the company found itself sitting with almost $100 billion in cash.

Once again, just because a company does one thing that you like such as pay dividends or have a low price to earnings ratio (P/E) does not mean that you should just automatically invest in it. That would be a very unwise decision that I advise all of my readers not to make.

Stock Splits

There are generally two scenarios when a company will decide to do a stock split. The first will be to decrease the price of its' stock to make it more attractive to new investors, and the other would be a reverse stock split to increase the price of a stock to make more attractive.

The first scenario, which is to decrease the stock price to make it more attractive would happen if the stock price has grown rapidly and the price no longer appears attractive to new and mainly amateur investors. The company would usually perform a 2 for 1 stock split. This would give all investors 2 shares for each 1 share that they currently own, and at the same time it would reduce the stock price in half. This doesn't add any profit or gain to the stock, but only makes it more attractive.

For example, let's say that the high demand for oil raised Exxon Mobil's stock price to $150 a share. This price is considered relatively high and the company would probably decide to do a 2 for 1 stock split. This would reduce the stock price to $75 while doubling the amount of shares that a particular investor currently has, which doesn't affect the value of the stock owned by the investor.

Let's say Denise owned 10 shares of the stock at $150 a share for a total value of $1,500. After the 2 for 1 stock split, Denise would then own 20 shares of the stock valued at the split price of $75 per share leaving her total value at $1,500. All the stock split did was make the stock price more attractive to new and normally amateur investors.

The other scenario that would lead a company to do a stock split is if the stock price is relatively low and unattractive. This would be the case if the stock price is very low and no one wants to invest in it because they think the low stock price makes it appear that it is a poor performing company, sometimes when it is actually not the case.

In this case, a company would generally do a reverse stock split. Let's say that because of all the losses and battles with union organizers that General Motor's stock price decreased to $2.00 a share. At this point, many investors would think the company is getting close to being de-listed from the New York Stock Exchange, and possibly headed toward bankruptcy. To help ease fears of investors, the company may decide to do a 1 for 10 stock split.

A 1 for 10 stock split would multiply the stock price by 10 making the value $20.00 a share versus $2.00, and it would reduce or divide the number of shares owned by 10. For example, let's say that Tina owned 100 shares of General Motor's stock at $2.00 per share for a total value of $200.00. After the company performed the 10 for 1 reverse stock split, Tina then would only own 10 shares of the stock that is now valued at $20.00 a share thus leaving her total value at $200.00.

Stock splits are universally common for profitable companies during extended economic expansions where stock prices are generally rapidly increasing across the board. During the economic expansion of the late 90's if was common for a blue chip company to perform a stock split once a year or every two years to keep the stock price from appearing unattractive.

Day Trading

Day trading is very popular and is usually done by all types of people with all different goals. Some people goals are to get rich quick, while others may be to flip their $3,000 tax return. Whatever the purpose, day trading can help you achieve your goals if done correctly, while if done incorrectly as it usually is, can clean you out and make you wish you never even heard of the stock market.

Day trading stocks can be compared to flipping real estate, as you buy a stock at a perceived low price, in hopes that you will be able to quickly sell it moments later, or at least later in the day ("day trading") at a profit. Sometimes this is achieved and sometimes it isn't, and it usually depends on the investment savvy of the day trader.

It is common to day trade with stocks that have a large daily volume, as all stocks don't sell large amounts everyday, and it is hard to day trade with a stock that doesn't have a daily demand. For the record, most stocks that are traded on the New York Stock Exchange and on NASDAQ have a pretty high trading volume, as it's one of the criteria to be listed on their exchanges.

It is also very common to day trade stocks that fluctuate very often. For example, if a company's stock price went from $10 to $12 and back again on a daily basis for two weeks straight, many day traders will consider investing (or gambling) in this stock in order to take advantage of the large range of fluctuation.

I don't recommend new investors to day trading because it is sometimes more emotional than rational, and new investors usually haven't learned to control their emotions when it comes to investing their money. Learning to control your emotions in relation to your finances usually takes some time maturing, loosing money, and watching the cycle of companies as well as the economy and seeing the short and long term effects of everything that happens.

I've lost my fair share of money day trading, as I didn't control my emotions and let fear take me out of good stocks, usually at prices that where less than the market value. As I matured and saw the business and stock price cycle that generally repeats itself over and over, I became more confident and starting making profits on some of my day trades.

Now a days, I will only day trade unintentionally, as I might buy a company that increases dramatically in value that same day, which will entice me to sell and take my quick profits.

Probably the biggest reason that I don't recommend purposely day trading for new investors, is because many times an amateur investor will buy a company with the purpose of day trading that they would've not purchased if they were not intending to day trade.

I truly believe that everyone at least sub-consciously has some sort of investment philosophy, and a lot of times when attempting to day trade, people will completely disregard their philosophy when the emotion that we all sometimes have "greed" takes over and a chance for a quick profit is hoped for.

I can definitely testify to that, as I lost several thousand dollars letting greed take precedent over my investment philosophy that came from profession industry training of being a former licensed financial advisor.

One day I was watching the stock of a small cap company that was rising about 20% every minute for about 15 minutes straight. As the stock price climbed steadily, I became very tempted to buy some and make a quick profit. My wife who was sitting at her desk next to mine even screamed at me to buy some, which was a totally emotional decision as she knew very little about stocks and investing. I broke my own rules and decided to buy some stock of a company that was rising rapidly, but didn't have any revenues, let alone any profit.

It was a bad emotional decision that cost me thousands. About ten minutes after I purchased the stock, the price started to decline, only it was decreasing at a much faster rate than it had increased, and by the time I was able to sell mine, I lost about 90% of the money I had invested. So the moral of this story is to not base investment decisions off emotion, especially when attempting to day trade, and if you're not 100% sure that you have your emotions in check, don't even think about day trading.

Summary of Chapter

As I stated earlier in the chapter, investing in stocks can be a very important piece of a well put together investment plan if used properly. I do not recommend stocks as a main course to any meal (investment portfolio), just as society wouldn't recommend corn as the main course of a real meal.

They say knowledge is power, and with the information you learned in this chapter, you should now know more about stocks than everyone in your family and possibly everyone in your neighborhood as well. Just remember to do more thinking than feeling and you should be alright. For more information on stock investing, visit the world popular www. BlackBusinessSmart.blogspot.com.

CHAPTER 6
WHAT YOU NEED TO KNOW ABOUT INVESTING IN BONDS

When I was putting together the outline for this book, I was having a huge debate within myself on rather or not I should include a chapter on bonds. I was having this debate because I'm not a big fan of bonds, and I couldn't see myself ever owning any, as I don't think they are a good investment for active and knowledgeable investors.

For the record I just don't like them, and I feel that if I would never own any of them myself, then I shouldn't recommend them to my readers. I thought about it for a few seconds before I came to a conclusion on the matter.

I decided to teach you the basics about them, while giving you my true opinion about them at the same time and let you know that I wouldn't buy them. However, I don't want to confuse anyone into thinking that they (bonds) are bad investments, because that's not the case, I just don't think that they make good investments. It's a difference.

Bonds are usually for retired people who are not active investors, or others who want to be able to say that they are investors, but don't want any risk to go with it. It is often said that bonds are for the more risk adverse people, while stocks and other investments are for those willing to take a chance.

I don't necessarily agree with this statement 100%, as I follow Robert Kiyosaki's philosophy and determine the level of risk of a particular investment by the level of knowledge that the investor has on that subject. For example, if you know a ton about real estate investing, than it is very little risk involved for you. On the other hand, if you know nothing about the real estate, your investing experience will be full of risk, and you may make a mistake that's hard to recover from.

What Are Bonds?

A bond is a contract (will be discussed in a later chapter) between the issuer and the investor. The investor borrows money to the issuer, which can be a corporation, the United States government, or a municipal board. In return for borrowing your money to the issuer, they agree to pay you a fixed amount of money, which is usually based on a percentage, for a certain period of time before they give you your money back.

For example, let's say Tania bought a bond from Wal-Mart for $5,000 that pays her 5% a year for 7 years. In "bond" talk, she really borrowed Wal-Mart $5,000 for 7 years, and they are going to pay her a 5% yield each year for 7 years. Each year for 7 years they would pay her $250 (5% of $5,000) per year until the end of the 7 years, and that's when they would just pay her the original $5,000 that she borrowed them back.

I don't like the idea of tying up my money for this long, while getting so little in return. This picture does look a little better when considering much larger dollar amounts, as we move to the next example.

Let's say that Tania won the lottery and bought a $5 million bond from General Motors. With all the trouble that they've had lately, they have to pay investors much higher yields to compensate for the risk, and they gave her a 9% yield on a 7 year bond. In this scenario, they would pay her $450,000 (9% of $5 million) a year for 7 years. In this scenario, I agree that a bond doesn't look that bad, but I figured that most people reading this book won't be in a position to invest $5 million into a bond.

My strong opinion of dislike for bonds is mainly geared toward investing small dollar amounts in them, like the first scenario of Tania and only getting so little back. I would much rather advise someone with only $5,000 to invest in a piece of real estate that should make them tens of thousands in profit over those same seven years.

Par Value of A Bond

The par value (which is also used interchangeably with face value) of a bond is the amount that will be paid to the investor when the bond matures. This amount is usually the same amount that was originally borrowed to the issuer by the investor, but can be different depending on the terms that were agreed to.

For example, let's say Tania bought a 5 year $1,000 bond from Exxon Mobil with a 5% yield. In addition to the $50 (5% of $1,000) a year that she would receive from Exxon Mobile, at the end of the 5 years, Tania would then receive her $1,000 in full that she originally borrowed Exxon Mobil. That $1,000 would be considered the par or face value.

Premiums & Discounts

Just as stocks can be traded on the open market, so can bonds. Also, just as the price that you sell a stock for may be different from the price that you paid, so can be the case when selling bonds.

Not all bonds that are taken out are held to maturity (the end of the loan period). In fact, many of them are sold on the secondary market at either a premium or discount years before the maturity date.

When a bond sells at a premium, it is sold for more than the par or face value of the loan. For example, a $1,000 bond selling at a premium might sell for $1,200. Bonds are generally sold at a premium if the bond has a higher interest rate or "yield" than what is currently being offered on the market.

For example, If Kela purchased a $1,000 bond with a yield of 8% when interest rates were high, and then a year later the best rate being offered for new bonds is 5%, Kela would be able to sell her bond at a premium (for more than the $1,000 she paid for it) as it is paying a higher interest rate or yield than what is currently being offered on the market.

On the flip side of the token, a bond could also be sold at a discount. When a bond sells at a discount it is sold for less than the face or par value of the loan. Bonds are usually sold at a discount when the yield (interest rate) on it is less than what is currently being sold on the market. .

For example, let's say Kela purchased a $1,000 bond with a yield of 4%, and 9 months later the interest rates being offered for bonds is 7%. If Kela wanted to sell her bond before the maturity date, she would have to sell it for less than the face value, as no one will want to buy a 4% bond for the same price that they can buy a 7% bond for. It wouldn't make sense. She would probably end up selling her bond for $700 or $800 as the 3% difference in her bond's interest rate (yield) and what the market is currently offering would cause for her to take a deep discount.

Bond Ratings

When investing, the reward of the investor is generally determined by the level of risk that is assumed. The higher the risk, the higher the potential reward must be, and vice versa. If there is little risk for the investor, the investor generally gets little reward. This is true with most investments and bonds are no exception.

The amount of risk that the investor assumes when borrowing a company or government entity money, will determine the interest rate (yield) given with the bond. If the company that is issuing the bond has had losses over the last couple quarters, then their bonds are considered riskier and must give higher yields (interest rates) to compensate for the high amount of risk.

On the other hand, if the US government is issuing the bond, there is very little risk assumed by the investor as they are considered the most stable entity in the world. In this case the investor would have to accept a below average interest rate since there is practically no risk involved.

To help investor's measure the amount of risk associated with each bond, Moody's and Standard & Poor's are two very prominent companies that rate the quality of each company's bond.

These two companies generally divide the risk of each bond between investment grade and speculative. Obviously the investment grade bonds have lower interest rates (yields) and the junk bonds have much higher interest rates (yields) to compensate for the additional risk.

With Moody's, the best grade that is given for the highest quality bond is Aaa, and then it proceeds with Aa, A, and Baa for investment grade bonds. Their junk bonds proceed in this following order:Ba, B, Caa, Ca, C. The lower the grade, the higher the yield (interest rate) that must be paid to attract investors.

With Standard and Poor's, their bond grades from best quality to worst are AAA, AA, A, BBB for investment grade, and BB, B, CCC, CC, CC, C, D for junk bonds. As they carry much higher interest rates (yields) then investment grade (high quality) bonds, junk bonds are often called high yield bonds.

Summary of Chapter

When this chapter first started, it may have appeared that I was anti-bonds. The truth is that I am not anti-bonds, but I did make it appear that way intentionally. The reason is because there are much better things to do with your money if you're trying to get rich, then buying bonds.

Although I've gained a ton of patience over the last few years, bonds just move too slow for me. I like money, and I like it fast, and that's why after you finish this book you will hear that I have another book about to release days after. Investing in bonds is not for a poor man, as it will only help you stay poor.

On the other hand, if you are rich and want to live off of steady assets, I think bonds may make a very good investment for you if you're investing at least $2 million and receiving a minimum of a 5% yield (interest rate). This way you know to expect $100,000 a year for the life of the bond, and then you can expect to receive your $2 million at the end of the life of the bond.

Like I said before, investment choices should be decided considering all factors including but not limited to your investment goals, risk tolerance, ambition, and most of all investment knowledge. For more information on investing in bonds, visit the world popular www.BlackBusinessSmart. blogspot.com.

CHAPTER 7
WHAT YOU NEED TO KNOW ABOUT BUSINESS ENTITIES

Besides the investing techniques we discussed in earlier chapters, there are many other legitimate ways to build wealth in this country, and by far the most famous strategy is by starting your own business. Not everyone is willing take this risk, as the level of risk is directly correlated to the high potential for reward.

In fact, the definition of entrepreneur is "someone who takes a risk and starts a business". So it isn't a secret that there is a big risk starting a business, and it also isn't a secret that the two richest men in the world have started them, namely Bill Gates with Microsoft, and Warren Buffet with Berkshire Hathaway.

As I uttered in a earlier chapter, I believe that the level of risk associated with something all depends on the level of knowledge the investor has in that particular business or investment. For example, if the founder of Nike decided to start another shoe company, it wouldn't be very much risk to him, as he has the experience from building one of the largest shoe companies in the world. While at the same time, if he tried to start a hair salon franchise, it would be much more risk associated for him, as his experience level on this topic is likely to be slim to none.

Starting and building a successful business can be one of the most rewarding feelings that a person ever experiences. Building a profitable business gives a person great feeling of accomplishment, in addition to wealth that can be passed down from generation to generation.

However, all of this potential for reward does come with the equal amount of risk, and large potential for failure. Approximately 80% of small businesses fail within the first five years, and then 90% of that reaming 20% fails within the next fives years. These can be very intimidating numbers to some people, while being used as motivation for others.

These numbers can be dramatically decreased with proper preparation before starting a business by doing research, shadowing other professionals in the industry, and definitely by reading all you can. I was once taught when I was younger that proper preparation prevents poor performance. With this in mind, it is scary to think of all of the people out there that start a business without putting together a sound business plan (will be discussed in a later chapter), and without any experience in that field.

Another thing that many entrepreneurs fail to do is select the appropriate business entity for their type of business. At first glance this may not sound very serious, but it definitely is. Certain entities will protect your personal assets such as your house and savings, while forming a business with other entities will put all of your personal possessions at risk in case something went wrong financially or criminally involving your business.

Selecting the appropriate entity is very important when attempting to build a successful business, as it may protect your personal belongings from lawsuits, both righteous and unrighteous ones that may be brought against you and your business. Besides building a strong business plan (that outlines your choice of entity anyway), I believe that carefully selecting the appropriate entity is the most important thing for any entrepreneur.

In today's litigious society, there are thousands of lawsuits being filed daily. Some of these lawsuits are legit, while many of them are people trying to get rich quick with a phony claim. Also, some of these lawsuits are being filed against the actual owner of the business, while many others, due to the choice of entity by the entrepreneur are filed against the business only, and can't go after any of the entrepreneur's personal belongings.

As a married man, I can truly say that a person's wife won't understand why she has to give up her 4 karat wedding ring because of a lawsuit brought forth because of possible negligence done by one of her husband's employees. Although this sounds horrifying, it is done constantly and mainly because of people not doing proper research and just forming the easiest entity there is, due to a lack of patience.

Sometimes when a person wants to make money, they loose sight of everything else that they are involved in, or become very limited in what they see. This is especially the case with young entrepreneurs who have created a very good product, or who have come up with a brilliant plan. Often after the concept of the business has been created, the entrepreneur will often see only see dollars signs and the potential profits of the idea.

This in return causes many entrepreneurs to loose sight of some of the most important things when starting a business, namely putting together a solid well thought out business plan, and selecting the appropriate entity. When doing these two things correctly, it definitely increases the entrepreneur's chance for success.

To help you with this, I will give you a list and details of the most popular entity choices available, such as the C Corporation, S Corporation, Limited Liability Company (LLC), Limited Liability Partnership (LLP), General Partnership, and the Sole Proprietorship.

C Corporation

What does Wal-Mart, Home Depot, General Motors, Nike, Mc Donald's, Exxon Mobil, Intel, Microsoft, Target, Ford, Lucent, Oracle, and every other company traded on the New York Stock Exchange and NASDAQ have in common? The answer is that they are all C-Corporations.

C Corporations are the most popular entity for large businesses and small businesses who plan to become large and publicly traded companies (those who sell stock to the general public). C Corporations have several benefits over all other types of entities, but a C Corporation is not for every business, as some businesses will serve better as either a Limited Liability Company (LLC) or S Corporation.

One of the biggest benefits of a C Corporation over all other entities is that the ownership interest (shares/stocks) can be easily traded (bough & sold) in the open market without any difficulty as long as there is a demand for the stock. This is the main reason why all of the large companies I named above that are traded on the stock market are C Corporations.

A C Corporation is considered its' own separate entity and can do many things that a person can, such as buy real estate, buy other businesses, get credit cards, sue people, and at the same time be sued. Of course a person or a group of people have to manage a corporation, but they are not considered to be the ones making the transaction when the corporation does something such as buy an investment property or sue someone.

Limited Liability

One of the best things about a C Corporation is that it has limited liability. This means that the only risk an investor has when investing in a C

Corporation is the investment that they made into the business. The owner (s) of a C Corporation can not be sued for negligence of the business, or for debts of the businesses unless personally agreed to do so.

Due to the limited liability factor, a C corporation can only be sued for the liabilities of the business and not the actual owners of a business. This adds a great level of protection, as with some entities all of the business's owners are held liable for any and all liabilities of the business, and can be sued for personal belongs such as their home, car, life savings, or even their wife's wedding rings to make right for wrong doings or debts of the business.

To give you an example of how this would work, I will give you the story of Kya. Kya was a published writer for several magazines, and she decided to start her own magazine called "My Life, Not Yours". Kya was smart and decided to seek legal advice, and after telling the attorney of all of her goals for the business, he recommended that she start a C Corporation.

About a year into the magazine, "My Life, Not Yours" had over 60 writers who wrote from time to time for the magazine. One month a particular writer decided to write about a rumor that he had heard about a famous celebrity as if he knew it was true. The magazine was nationwide, and the article about the celebrity created a large negative buzz about the celebrity, and was believed by the celebrity to be the reason why she didn't get a movie role that she had auditioned for.

This had made the celebrity furious and she was determined to get some payback. The first thing she thought about was suing the owner of the magazine. When she met with her lawyer about the issue, the celebrity's attorney notified her that he would not be able to sue the owner of the magazine, but only the magazine itself because it had limited liability protection as a C Corporation.

This of course made the celebrity even more upset, as she decided to get payback by saying bad things about the magazine and it's owner that weren't true on a late night talk show. After Kya spoke with her lawyer about the situation, he advised her to file a law suit against the celebrity for slander asking for $5 million for the magazine, and another $5 million for Kya's personal damages

When the celebrity heard about this, she was enraged as she was personally being sued by both Kya and by the magazine. She had two slander law suits against her for the same action, as Kya's attorney felt that the celebrity's action hurt the reputation of both Kya and the Magazine.

Instead of turning this story into a long novel, the point of this story is to show how a corporation can be sued, how it can sue others, and how it provides limited liability protection for its owner(s).

Piercing The Corporate Veil

In some instances the limited liability of a corporation and its owner(s) can be disregarded. When the limited liability aspect of a corporation is disregarded, it is legally called "piercing the corporate veil". Piercing the corporate veil means that the owner(s) of a corporation are being held personally liable for the actions or debts of the business. This generally only happens in situations of misconduct where the owner(s) have done something fraudulently, deceiving, or something that went against corporation laws.

Actions that can cause the allowance of piercing the corporate veil would include the owner(s) commingling business and personal funds, deceiving someone to do business with the corporation, while thinking they are doing business with a person, and when a business is intentionally set up to take a loss for tax purposes or unable to pay its bills or a regular basis. These are all common reasons that will allow piercing the corporate veil and remove an owner(s) rights to limited liability.

Taxation

As its' own entity, a corporation must file its' own tax return separately of the individual owners. As with some limited liability entities, if a corporation takes a loss for the year it can not pass that loss down to the company's owners, but is only considered a loss for the business. Business that can pass down losses are considered pass though entities and the C Corporation is not one of them.

Tax rates in which C Corporations pay taxes on is generally a lot less than what someone would pay with a pass though entity, as a pass though entity (if has profits) would pay taxes at the owner(s) individual tax rate.

For example, for the first $50,000 in profits of a corporation, the tax rate is only 15%. The next $25,000 ($50k-$75k) would be taxed at 25%, and the next $25,000 ($75k-$100k) would be taxed at 34%. This will generally save a business a lot of money if retaining income, as it is normally less than a persons' individual tax rate of 28 to 50%

One of the downsides to the way corporations are taxed is the fact that they are often double taxed. What double taxation means is that a corporation must pay taxes on any profits it earned, and if the company decides to pay out any dividends to it's owners, they will also be taxed on their share of profits received, thus causing double taxation.

This is very unfavorable among many entrepreneurs and is the reason why many of them stray away from C Corporations until they grow and decide to go public. It is important to note than a business can start out as one entity and then switch to another with the proper filing of paperwork.

Forming A C-Corporation

A C Corporation is formed by filing what is known as "the articles of incorporation" with the secretary of state. The articles of incorporation would include such items as the company's reserved (reserved with secretary of state to check for availability) name, purpose of the business, board of directors, and the company's Bylaws.

The Bylaws of a corporation outline the rules of the business, and how they are to handle corporate affairs such as shareholder and board of director meetings. The bylaws also generally list the responsibilities of each officer and director, as well as the proper procedure to remove them from office if ever needed.

Each state charges a different fee for filing the articles of incorporation, so it's important to get those numbers ahead of time from your local secretary of state's office.

A resident agent also must be designated in the state that the corporation was organized in. The role of the resident agent is to accept law suits and complaints in case they are ever filed against your business. Many corporations use attorneys as their resident agents to assure themselves proper representation and response to any and all complaints.

The owner of a corporation could serve as their own resident agent if they live in the state that the business is formed in, otherwise an attorney is always a good option.

S Corporation

The S Corporation is very similar to the C Corporation. In fact, in order to have a S Corporation, one must form a C Corporation first. After incorporating into a C Corporation, the business owner(s) must then fill out form 2553 with the IRS in order to qualify for S Corporation status.

As with a C Corporation, a S Corporation also has limited liability protection from debts and wrong doings of the business and its' employees. The difference from a S Corporation and a C Corporation lies within it tax status, as well as it's restrictions.

Tax Status

A S Corporation is considered a pass through tax entity. This means that the owners of a S Corporation only file one tax return, which is opposite of a C Corporation, where the business has to file it's own tax return.

All profits or losses of a S Corporation pass down to its' owners. This means that if the business takes a loss (actual or paper), then the loss passes down to the owners personal tax return. For example, let's say Lisa started a part time business and formed it as a S Corporation that had a loss of $50,000 its' first year. Let's also say that Lisa still had her full time job of an engineer that paid her $60,000 a year. Because of the pass through tax status of a S Corporation, after deducting the $50,000 business loss from her $60,000 salary as an engineer, she would only pay taxes on $10,000 of income, as that would be her new adjusted gross income, minus or plus any other income or deductions.

This is a great benefit to forming a S Corporation, versus a C Corporation, as this is not allowed with a C Corporation. A loss with a C Corporation is considered a loss of the business and can not be passed down to its' owner(s).

S Corporation Restrictions

The S Corporation has several restrictions that make it unattractive depending on the goals of the business, and the way it is to be owned and controlled. The following are a few guidelines that may lead a person to form a C Corporation or a Limited Liability Company versus a S corporation as originally planned.

1.)   A S Corporation may not have more than 75 share-holders. This is one of the reasons a large business that has the intentions to go public (be traded on one of the major exchanges) shall not form a S Corporation, as most publicly traded companies have tens of millions of shares available to the public to be traded (bought and sold).

2.)   Corporations and many types of trust may not be share-holders of a S Corporation. This is another reason why a large company that plans to go public should not form a S Corporation. A large public company's stock is usually purchased by other companies, and it can't do that with a S Corporation.

3.)   A S Corporation may not have non US citizens as share-holders. This is another tough restriction of a S Corpo-ration, as many times venture capitalist and other inves-tors will be resident aliens, or may actually physically reside in another country.

4.)   A S Corporation may only have one class of stock. It can not have preferred and common stock, just one or the other. This is another pitfall of the S Corporation as some investors will want a different form of stock (ownership) than the general public, but will be unable to do so in a S Corporation as only one form of stock is allowed.

5.)   Profits and losses of a S Corporation must be split even-ly based on the percentage of ownership. This means that if one of the owners own 20% of the business, they can only receive 20% of the profits or losses of the com-pany

The S Corporation definitely does have its' benefits, as well as its potential cost, as forming one can heavily restrict who can invest in your business, thus ultimately controlling the way and how fast it grows.

Limited Liability Company (LLC)

In my opinion, the Limited Liability Company (LLC) is the best of both worlds. Out of all the entities it is my favorite one by far. The only time I wouldn't use a Limited Liability Company is if I was getting ready to take a business public (be traded on one of the major exchanges), and in that case I would be required to form a C Corporation.

The Limited Liability Company (LLC) has the limited liability protection of the C and S Corporations, as well as the pass through tax status of the S Corporation without all the crazy restrictions giving it the best of both worlds. The biggest difference from Limited Liability Company and a S Corporation is the way profits and losses can be divided.

As stated above, in a S Corporation, the profits and losses must be divided evenly based on the percentage of ownership. For example, if Tesha and Casandra own a S Corporation, they must split the profits or losses of the business 50/50. No other agreements can be worked out, even if agreed to in writing.

With a Limited Liability Company (LLC), the profits and losses can be distributed in any way the owners please. So if a particular investor will only invest if he gets 50% of the profits for the first two years, but he only owns 25% of the business, with a Limited Liability Company (LLC) this is perfectly attainable as long as it's agreed to in writing.

This is a big advantage over the S Corporation as well as the lack of restrictions that are applied to the Limited Liability Company (LLC).

Forming A Limited Liability Company

In order to form a Limited Liability Company, one must file the "Articles of Organization" with the secretary of state. There is a fee to file this, and it varies by state. The articles of organization include the company's name, purpose, resident agent, and if the business is Manager or Member managed.

With a LLC, manager managed means that one of the owners will have executive power over the business, while member managed means that multiple or all owners will have executive powers over the business.

The next form that must be put together (although not filed with the secretary of state) is the company's operating agreement. The operating agreement outlines the rules for operations of the business. It will generally list requirements for meetings, removing managers, process to transfer or sell ownership interest, and distribution of profits and losses. If the last part isn't included, then profits and losses must me divided evenly according to ownership percentages.

The Limited Liability Company (LLC) has a lot of benefits, and can be the perfect entity depending on the goals and objectives of the business and its' owner(s). Like I stated before, unless I plan on going public in the near future, in which case I would need a C Corporation, the LLC is my business entity of choice.

Limited Partnership

The limited partnership in my opinion is a half good and half bad entity. A Limited Partnership (LP) is a business that has at least one limited partner and at least one general partner. The reason I say a Limited Partnership is half good and half bad is because only the limited partner has limited liability of personal risk, whereas the general partner is at total risk and is held personally responsible for any debts or wrongdoings of the business.

The general partner(s) is the one that manages the business and has executive say over the business and its' day to day operations. The general partner is usually the one that found the business or in most cases was the primary investor. The general partner(s) have no limited liability protection of personal assets and can be wiped clean if the business has a large law suit against it.

The limited partner is considered a silent partner and has no say in day to day activity of the business. If a limited partner becomes actively involved in the business, they can loose their limited liability protection as only a general partner has the right to be involved in the day to day management of a limited partnership.

The limited partner is usually a minority investor in the business and wants nothing to do with the operations of the business because they don't want to loose their limited liability protection.

To give a clear illustration of how this works, I'll give you the story of Bob and George. Bob and George had a great idea and they started a limited partnership. Bob was cocky because he had a business degree and wanted to be in charge of the business, thus the general partner. However, George was street smart and knew that as the limited (silent) partner he would enjoy limited liability protection in case something went wrong, so he quickly agreed.

Six months into the business, one of their employees spit in a customers face during a heated argument. The customer than filed a multi-million dollar law suit against the business and won in court as the incident was recorded on tape. As the general partner of the business, Bob was handed the bill as a personal debt, while nothing was ever said to George about any debts. George as the limited partner was not at all personally responsible for any debts of the business.

Forming A Limited Partnership

To form a Limited Partnership, you must file a "certificate of limited partnership with the secretary of state. The certificate of limited partnership generally includes the partnership name, exact description of the business, resident agent, general partner information, duration of the business, and reasons for dissolving the business.

A Limited Partnership must also structure a limited partnership agreement. The limited partnership agreement list the duties of the general partner, limited partner's voting rights, and guidelines for transferring or selling ownership interest.

General Partnership and Sole Proprietorship

A General Partnership and a Sole Proprietorship are the two worst business entities known to man when it comes to personal asset protection. A General Partnership is a partnership with all general partners and no limited partners. So this means that everyone involved in a General Partnership is at risk of personal assets being seized to satisfy the debts of the business, thus no one in a General Partnership is safe.

A Sole Proprietorship is a one person owned business, where the owner takes full personal liability for the business. With all the entity options available I don't understand why people are still forming these two forms of business. In my personal opinion, a person should be committed for forming one of these, especially if their business will have contact with people.

Forming a General Partnership & Sole Proprietorship

DON'T FORM ONE!!!

Summary of Chapter

When picking an entity for your business it is important to choose one that will benefit your needs, as if you plan to go public soon, it would be unwise to form a limited liability company or a limited partnership that can't be easily traded or exchanged on the stock market, unlike with a C Corporation.

Also, one must consider the need for tax breaks and deductions to personal income, if the business is expected to take a paper loss (a loss only on paper for tax purposes), or even an actual loss for that matter. Many things must be considered, as a loss with a C Corporation can't be passed down to personal income, but this can be done with an S Corporation, limited liability company or general and limited partnerships. This can also be done with sole proprietorships, but due to the risk involved, I wouldn't recommend forming a sole proprietorship unless your life depended on it.

And please remember to never form a Sole Proprietorship or General Partnership. Also know that if you start a business with another person(s) and haven't filed for a specific entity, then you have automatically started a general partnership. And if you are starting a business by your self and haven't filed for a specific entity, then you have automatically started a Sole Proprietorship.

I don't usually give examples in the chapter summary, but this last point needs an example to make sure you're clear. Let's say you start selling candy out of your apartment. You don't think it's that serious so you don't form a legal entity with the secretary of state, and one of the kids you sold candy to gets sick and dies from some candy that was purchased from you. Guess what? You are personally liable as you are operating a Sole Proprietorship by default

In this case, if the family of the child decides to sue you, you can be wiped out of everything you have, or anything you may gain in the future.

So remember: C Corporations are good. S Corporations are good. Limited Liability Company's are my favorite. Limited Partnerships are half good and half bad, while General Partnerships and Sole Proprietorship offer no protection and are tragedies waiting to happen. For more information on business entities, visit www.BlackBusinessSmart.blogspot.com.

CHAPTER 8
WHAT YOU NEED TO KNOW ABOUT BUSINESS PLANS

Statistics show that 80% of small businesses fail within their first three to five years. This can be an alarming number, not only to potential entrepreneurs, but to society as well since small businesses employ about 50% of all employees and create close to 90% of all new jobs.

There are many reasons that contribute to why small businesses fail, including but not limited to ignoring the competition, ineffective marketing, ignoring consumers' needs, incompetent employees, poor location, cash flow problems, and procrastination on behalf of the management staff.

Of the reasons listed, the two that calls for the most attention are location, and the lack of meeting consumers' needs. Many entrepreneurs when looking for a location to start their business don't take into account such simple things as the area's traffic, which is vital to your success. You can have the best restaurant in the world, but if no one ever hears about it or at least drives pass it, then that business may be one of those establishments that fail within the first three to five years.

Also, an abundance of entrepreneurs don't take into account what the consumers in their area want to buy that's not already being provided to them at cost lower than their business can afford to beat. This also goes in line with ignoring the competition. For example, some small tire shops have opened up less than a half a mile from a Sam's Club. This makes little to no sense due to Sam's Club having tires that are priced far below what most small businesses can compete with, due to Wal-Mart's bulk buying power.

For some reason it is evident that a lot of aspiring businessmen and women don't take into account the simple things when considering starting a business and that is because they don't spend time doing or paying someone to help them do a solid business plan. Research shows that most people take more time to plan a vacation then they do to properly plan for their business, which is scary at the least.

Doing a thorough business plan would answer all of those unanswered questions for an entrepreneur, as well as those non-thought of questions, that make you say, "you know, I never thought of that". A sound business plan should include the following sections that are complete and full of exact detail:

1.) Executive Summary: The executive summary explains the objectives, goals, and mission statement of the business. This is similar to an introduction, as it will briefly discuss what's about to be read inside of the business plan. Generally when looking for funding, if the executive summary isn't strong, the rest of the business plan will either not be looked at, or in a best case scenario it will be breezed through.

2.) Ownership & Management: This section provides details on the type of business and management team the company will have. This section is very important, especially with Limited Liability Companies, and Limited Partnerships that can have different forms of management, and can be controlled fully by only one owner. In the case of a LLC it will detail if it's going to be manager managed and controlled by one of the owners, or member managed and controlled by all or multiple members.

3.) History of Company: This section gives detail of the history of the business if there is a history. Many business plans are done for a new business, while others are done on businesses that already exist that need funding for growing, or just want a clear direction of where the business is going. This section will talk about any obstacles that the business has overcome that likely may reappear in the future. As they say, history usually repeats itself.

4.) Products and Services: This section explains what products and services are being offered by the business. This section will also give information on the need for the product or service, and any other reason why the owners of the business expect this product or service to be profitable. This section needs to be very detail as most businesses live and die based on the product or service being offered by the business. If you don't have a needed or highly demanded product or service before starting a business, I recommend you not starting one.

5.) Locations & Facilities: This section gives the location(s) of the business. This section is one of the most critical parts as location is one of the main focuses of any solid marketing plan. A good location could mean a lot of free flowing business, while a bad location could be the downfall for a business with a great product or service. In business, you location needs to be visible as well as accessible by your target market (the specific people you are trying to sell to).

6.) Sourcing: This section explains the cost of the benefits being offered. It will detail the price that the business is being charged for manufacturing of merchandise, or for services that are being offered on behalf of the business. This can be very critical also, as if the price that you pay to bring a product to market is more than what consumers are willing to pay for it, this is a recipe for disaster and should be spotted before investing thousands or millions of dollars into a business.

7.) Technology: This section explains if the business owns any patents, copyrights, or trademarks that will help the business become profitable. A lot of times the technology that the business has patented will be the difference from a successful business and one that can't keep good data of past customers. I say past customers because with out proper follow up, that's what they'll generally become.

8.)   Market Segmentation: This section divides the market place into workable segments. It should break down each niche or market that will be targeted by the business. It will describe the order of marketing attacks, and the affect that each attack will have on the market. This is very important, as if no market is targeted, often no market will become established.

9.)   Industry Analysis: This section is one of the most important sections, as it may tell you ahead of time that you shouldn't start the business or at least not in the location that you were considering. This section explains who the competitors are in your market as well as in the neighborhood of the business. Similar to what I said earlier, if you are starting a tire shop, and when doing the industry analysis in your business plan you realize that Sam's Club is only blocks away, this should cause you to re-direct your business plan and change locations.

10.)   Competitor's Buying Patterns: This section will explain the logic and reasoning to the competitors buying style. This is very important, as knowing what your competitors are doing right, could help you do the same things right as well.

11.)   Marketing Strategy: This is probably the most important section of a solid business plan, as it will address exactly how you will make sales and ultimately profits. It tells how you will implement the focus of your business and get your product or service known to your target market, and ultimately the entire world.

12.)   Pricing Strategy: This section is generally combined with the marketing strategy as it shows the current price list and discount structure of the products or services being offered by your business. It will show proposed margins (difference from sale price and cost of item) as well as detail any loss leader items that will be sold below cost to attract customers into your business and ultimately do a lot of impulse shopping.

13.) Advertising Strategy: This section is also usually combined in the marketing strategy section. It will describe exactly how you plan to spread the news about your business with a close estimate of how much each action will cost, and the exact dollars expected from each advertisement, which is also known as "ROI" or return on investment.

14.) Strategic Alliances: The strategic alliance section will show if you plan to join forces with another company in order to strengthen the position of your business. Aligning your business with another company can be a great benefit for you as it can expose your business to new markets that it may have never been exposed to.

15.) Break Even Analysis: This section explains how much income is needed to recoup cost incurred. In a business that has a product for sale, this section will show exactly how many pieces are need to be sold in order to break even, and ultimately to make a profit.

16.) Final Summary: Wraps up the main details of why your business is worth investing into, and why it will be successful. This section will be a reflection of some of the best ideas of the business plan, and will remind the reader of every section that caught their attention.

Summary of Chapter

Preparing a solid business plan is essential for any business that plans to grow and be successful. Many people think that a business plan is just to help them plan their business, but just as important it will often tell them that starting that particular business is a bad idea and if heeded to will save the entrepreneur a ton of time and money.

Even if you need to pay someone to help you, I ask that you please don't start a business with out a good business plan. There are many counseling firms listed in the yellow pages that can help you put together a solid business plan. It may cost you several hundred to a few thousand dollars, but it is much better than starting a business that will go bankrupt six weeks into it. For more business advice, visit the world popular www. BlackBusinessSmart.blogspot.com.

CHAPTER 9
WHAT YOU NEED TO KNOW ABOUT MARKETING

In my opinion, marketing is the most important aspect in building a profitable world class business for any entrepreneur, and definitely the most critical section in a solid business plan. If a consumer doesn't know to demand your product or service, then they generally won't, because they can't if they aren't aware that it exists.

Marketing is the tool that is used to introduce your product or service to the consumer, and ultimately build a "household" brand name for that product or service. Some of the most reputable companies in the world have used solid marketing plans to build their brand name, and eventually place their business in a class above the competition.

For example, Nike who is the largest athletic shoemaker in the world got that way from great marketing and promotions. In the early to mid-eighties Nike practically made Michael Jordan, who became the greatest player to ever play the game of basketball, the face of Nike. At the time, Michael Jordan gave Nike a reputation for helping athletes "fly" or stay in the air a little longer than everyone else. With that, they made a fortune with their Nike Air brand, even if the shoe wasn't directly related to Michael Jordan.

Even if a person couldn't afford to get the Michael Jordan Nike shoe, they still wanted to be associated with Nike in any way they could, and shortly thereafter, Nike was the shoe of choice for both young and old athletic consumers. Recently over the last few years, Nike has done a great job of grabbing other talent, such as Lebron James and offering him a mega $90 million endorsement deal.

Many outsiders didn't understand why they paid him so much money, and that is because they didn't understand marketing and the importance of a business branding their product. Nike understands that even if the Lebron James shoe doesn't make them $90 million in profit over the term of the deal, they will make their profit off of the branding that he will continue to provide for the shoe maker in associating Nike with world class athletes.

This concept will surely make them much more than $90 million over time, and will be the main reason why Nike maintains its' position as the number one athletic shoe maker. Many other shoe companies don't believe in paying top dollar for world class athletes as they only consider what that athlete will provide as far as their particular shoe sales, versus the bigger picture, which is the branding effect their affiliation will have for the shoe company.

Understanding this concept is the same as understanding marketing. According to The American Marketing Association, "marketing is the process of planning and executing the conception, pricing, promotion, and distribution of ideas, goods, and services to create exchanges that satisfy individual and organizational objectives." In my own words, marketing is the process of creating public awareness of a particular product or service and in some cases an entire business.

It is important to note that marketing is more than just advertising, the same way as a house is more than just a kitchen. Advertising is indeed a part of marketing, but the concept of marketing expands far beyond just advertising, just as a house expands far beyond just a kitchen.

Target Market

When marketing, the main goal is generally to reach a specific market. A market can be described as a collection of existing or potential customers who have the desire and ability to buy a specific product or service. The specific market that is sought after by a particular business or marketing plan is considered the target market.

Many businesses start out with a single target market that expands strategically in order to gain a larger market share. A good marketing plan will state a least one target market, as well as the effect that market will have on other markets once reached. Having a clearly defined target market is very important before starting any business, no matter if it is a product or service that you need to sell in order to make a profit.

A target market should include a group of people that have the desire and ability to buy a product or service. For example, if starting a restaurant that sells very large cheeseburgers, the target market could be overweight consumers who have a high demand or desire for such food items.

If starting a book publishing company that writes mostly business books, the target market could be business students and business schools as a whole. Once a target market is defined, the marketing plan should detail exactly how the product or service will get introduced to that market, and what will be done to persuade that market that the product that's being offered is worth the price that is being charged for that product.

Many different strategies can be implemented in order to successfully carry out a sound marketing plan such as mail advertising, telemarketing, news ad advertising, word of mouth, and television commercials to name a few.

Generally the target market of a business grows as the original market has been captured and generating the sales goals that were planned when the target market was defined. Often a new market will be introduced unintentionally. This can happen in many ways, but generally word of mouth will be the cause.

For example, let's say the target market of a book publishing company was urban women between the ages of 15 and 24. Because of the known relation between women and men in this age group, unintentionally, males in this age group could become a new market as they become curious of what their significant others are indulged in. At this point the company's marketing efforts would now expand to reach this male audience as well as the original target audience.

This could very well lead to another market being created, as the younger brothers of the older members of the 15 to 24 crowd may become curious of what their big brothers are reading. This could then lead to a whole new entire market of middle school age kids reading books published by this company that started out with the single target market of urban females ages 15 to 24.

When it comes to defining an initial target market, it should be a group that will likely openly receive your product or service, as well as a group that will have some sort of influence on another market. That way you can kill two birds with one stone, and expand into other markets without any direct attempts to do so.

On the contrary, not defining a target market is generally a recipe for failure as if no clear market it targeted, than no clear market will be sought after, leading to a very ineffective marketing campaign and entrepreneurial effort.

The Four P's

One of the best known marketing concepts in business is the Four P's. This is also commonly referred to as the controllable marketing factors, as it is the aspects of marketing that can be controlled by a company's marketing department. Not all marketing factors can be controlled by a company, as a lot of marketing is done by word of mouth, and consumer psychology or behavior often has a lot to do with consumer spending and awareness.

In business school, one of the first things learned in marketing class is the Four P's. The Four P's stands for product, price, promotion, and place. This is a very important concept, as they're the only factors that can be controlled by the business with the product or service to offer.

Product

The product or service that a company has to offer will generally make or break a business. You can have the best marketing in the world, but if the product isn't any good, then the product won't be purchased, and if it is, it will generally be complained about and not only not purchased again by the person that originally bought the product, but also not bought by whoever was on the other end of the complaints.

The product or service that is offered is the vital point of any business idea. Before doing any type of business or marketing plan, a good product or service that has a high demand needs to be created. To keep it simple, without a good product there is no business or at least there shouldn't be.

Price

The price of a product is very critical. Just as having a good product is very important, the price of that product is equally as important, as a poorly priced product can be just as bad as having a poor product itself.

Many times a company will have a great product or service to offer, but it will be priced without consideration of the spending ability of the target market. For example, if I was writing a book on the steps to escape poverty, it would be unwise to price this book at $39, as many people in poverty wouldn't be able to afford spending that much money on a book, especially when the need to get food is the more immediate concern.

On the other hand, a great product can be under priced and cause a business to fail. When deciding on the price of a product, one needs to consider all cost associated with producing and promoting that product, as well as the contribution that the sales of that product will have toward the general overhead of the business.

When evaluating the price of a product, if it appears that the product needs to be priced at a cost that is higher than what the competition is currently selling the same product for, it generally is a strong sign that the business idea needs to be re-evaluated. When this happens, it means that the consumer need that you are attempting to supply is already being met at a price that you can't afford to compete with.

Promotion

The proper promotion of a product is as equally important to properly pricing, as well as having a good product itself. A business can have the best product at the lowest price in the world, but if no one knows about it, it more than likely won't sell as someone can't request what they don't know exists.

For example, I can have a car dealership that sells Cadillac Escalade trucks for $500. That's right $500. This is obviously a great product at a ridiculously low price, but if no one knows about it, then chances are that I won't sell any unless someone stumbles upon my car dealership by accident.

Proper promotion creates consumer awareness of a particular product or service that is being offered. This is very important, because as I stated earlier a consumer can't attempt to consume something that they don't know exists.

Place

Similar to how having a good product with a proper price, and having good promotion is critical to the success of a business, so is the importance of having the product in the right place. A business can have the perfect product, with a similar price and great promotion, but if the product isn't in a place that can be easily accessed by the target market, then failure may be right around the corner.

For example, if I was selling high end dresses targeted toward wealthy consumers, it would be unwise to only have this product for sale in the inner city as it would create a barrier and possible hesitation for my target market to access my product. Having a product in the right place is very important, and can make or break a business idea or company as a whole.

When preparing a solid marketing plan, all four phases of the four p's must be heavily considered, as not one element may be ignored or lightly regarded. We've seen how any one can make or break a great business concept, even if the other three have been brilliantly put together.

Consumer Decision Making Process

When putting together a good marketing plan, it is very important to understand the psychology of a consumer as they decide to purchase a particular product or service. Many people don't think it's important to understand this, but they are tragically mistaken. The way I look at it is, if you know the process that's done by a consumer leading up to a purchase, then with the proper marketing, one can easily interfere with that process and find a way to make their product or service the selection of choice.

The first step in the consumer purchasing process is that they recognize that they have a need for a particular item or service. This can occur from waking up to the feeling of thirst, having a cough, finding an empty cereal box in the food closet, and many other things can trigger this recognition of a need.

After a particular need is recognized, consumers usually perform an internal search as they try to remember how they last for filled the same need when it emerged. If no good experiences exist, then the consumer will move on to do an external search and ask friends and family for information, as well as other sources that give information on the product or service that is being craved.

After the consumer has done their proper research, either mentally or physically on the computer, they will compare all of their reasonable options and look for the best value and all around choice. I was once told in psychology class as an undergraduate student that a person decides to have a relationship with someone or something by evaluating the benefits, the cost, and the availability of competing relationships. This is very similar to what a consumer does at this stage in the process. It may only take 5 seconds, but subconsciously all things will have been considered.

After evaluating the options available, the consumer will eventually come to a decision and make a purchase. At this point they will then decide who to buy it from, which is very important as a business needs to be ready to position itself to be the place where the product or service is purchased from. This isn't an easy task, but properly following the four p's will have a business at the top of a consumers' list.

After the purchase and consumption of a product, the consumer will generally create an opinion rather good or bad on the experience and store it mentally for later use when the same need re-appears in the future.

Word of Mouth

Word of mouth marketing is probably the best marketing there is. Word of mouth has been the bread and butter for many companies, especially underground music labels that don't get much or any radio play or spins on MTV. Believe it or not, word of mouth is practically inevitable as after a product is consumed, the opinion that is created is usually shared with anyone who will listen.

This is the case rather the opinion formed is positive or negative. Generally when the experience is negative, the consumer will tell many more people than they would if the experience had been a good one. It is sometimes true when they say that people feed off negative energy, both the deliverer of the information as well as the recipient.

Personally, everyone who reads this book and recommends it to all of their friends and family to help them advance their financial education, and ultimately financial situation, I find this as the perfect time to thank you. So Thank You!

80/20 Rule

The 80/20 Rule states that 80 percent of all sales and profits will come from 20 percent of the items or customers. This is very important to know as it helps you focus your business efforts on particular customers and products. Customers that do 80 percent of the spending deserve 80 percent of the attention from marketers and managers.

Likewise, an item or category of items that provides 80 percent of the sales should be given 80 percent of the attention, and should be strongly monitored to make sure that it is always in stock. Although all customers are important and should be treated with respect, it's not wise to spend a lot of time on customers who don't have the ability to do a large amount of purchases. Like I said before, if it don't make dollars, then it don't make sense.

Summary of Chapter

Marketing is a very important topic that must be covered before a business decides to open its' doors for operations. Without the proper marketing, although the doors of a business may be open, it is very likely that no one will enter as no one will probably know anything about the business, or at least not what the business has to offer versus the competition.

From defining a target market, to using careful consideration of the four p's, marketing can be the bread and butter of any business that has admirations to grow and become profitable. If no other part of a business plan is done before you start a business, I ask that you please at least do a solid marketing plan. For more information on expert marketing, visit the world popular <u>www.BlackBusinessSmart.blogspot.com</u>.

CHAPTER 10
WHAT YOU NEED TO KNOW ABOUT ACCOUNTING

When it comes to investing, there are certain accounting basics that must be known, and understood very well in order to prevent your investing efforts from becoming gambling, as that is the true title for the action that is done when an uneducated person attempts to invest.

This chapter isn't going to be about traditional accounting that would include talks about inventory and such topics, but is more about the accounting information needed to make intelligent investment decisions.

From time to time I hear people ignorantly talking about how certain companies have such a great stock or is a "must buy". Then when you ask them how much cash the company has on hand they turn dumbfounded. You then ask what are their quarterly liabilities compared to their cash on hand or quarterly income and they look at you even crazier. Why? Because they don't know. Most amateur investors invest on bad advice they've received from a salesman (financial advisor), or even worse, a hot stock tip.

To reduce the chances of buying a bad investment, one must educate themselves on the particulars of what makes a company healthy from a financial point of view. If you knew that a company had quarterly debt of $2 billion and quarterly sales of only $1.2 billion on average over the last two years, one might be a little more skeptical about becoming a shareholder.

This company is obviously loosing money on a regular basis. Once that happens it's not too long before talks of bankruptcy emerge, and after that, you can be sure of a declining stock price.

Before investing, it is important to learn where to find such vital information and how to determine rather it's good or bad from an investment point of view. This important information is public records for all publicly traded companies and can be found on the Yahoo! Finance page after entering the company's ticker symbol in for a stock quote.

In my opinion, the two most important sources of information are the balance sheet and the income statement. These two items basically tell an investor everything that is needed to know about the financials of a company. Their importance can be considered similar to checking the blood pressure or sugar level of a diabetic. In some situations, after looking at a company's balance sheet or income statement, it will warn you that the company needs some immediate medical attention as it may be dying slowly.

Balance Sheet

The balance sheet can be described as an x-ray of the financial condition of the company. It is divided into 3 sections: Assets, Liabilities, and Stockholders' Equity. The asset section shows how much cash the company has on hand, value of any investments, value of all accounts receivable (money owed to the company), and value of all other assets.

The liability section shows everything that the company owes. This will include all accounts payable, long term debt and any other dollar amount that the company owed someone at the time of the x-ray. This section is very important and combined with the asset section lets you know if the company has enough money to pay its' bills if all revenues stopped coming in (which is unlikely with most large companies).

In my opinion the Stockholders Equity portion isn't as important as the first two sections but does include such items as treasury stock (company stock that the company has purchased back from the open market), and retained earnings (all money kept by the company after paying expenses and dividends).

Carefully looking at a company's balance sheet, can stop someone from making a very bad investment decision, as knowing how much cash a company has versus the amount of short term debt can be the difference from success and failure especially when investing in a small cap company.

Below is a recent copy of Wal-Mart's balance sheet as copied from the Yahoo! Finance page.

PERIOD ENDING	31-Jan-06	31-Jan-05	31-Jan-04
All Numbers Are In Thousands			
Assets			
Current Assets			
Cash And Cash Equivalents	6,414,000	5,488,000	5,199,000
Short Term Investments	-	-	-
Net Receivables	2,662,000	1,715,000	1,254,000
Inventory	32,191,000	29,447,000	26,612,000
Other Current Assets	2,557,000	1,841,000	1,356,000
Total Current Assets	**43,824,000**	**38,491,000**	**34,421,000**
Long Term Investments	-	-	-
Property Plant and Equipment	79,290,000	68,567,000	58,530,000
Goodwill	12,188,000	10,803,000	9,882,000
Intangible Assets	-	-	-
Accumulated Amortization	-	-	-
Other Assets	2,885,000	2,362,000	2,079,000
Deferred Long Term Asset Charges	-	-	-
Total Assets	**138,187,000**	**120,223,000**	**104,912,000**
Liabilities			
Current Liabilities			
Accounts Payable	40,178,000	35,107,000	31,051,000
Short/Current Long Term Debt	8,648,000	7,781,000	6,367,000
Other Current Liabilities	-	-	-
Total Current Liabilities	**48,826,000**	**42,888,000**	**37,418,000**
Long Term Debt	30,171,000	23,669,000	20,099,000
Other Liabilities	-	-	-
Deferred Long Term Liability Charges	4,552,000	2,947,000	2,288,000
Minority Interest	1,467,000	1,323,000	1,484,000
Negative Goodwill	-	-	-
Total Liabilities	**85,016,000**	**70,827,000**	**61,289,000**
Stockholders' Equity			
Misc Stocks Options Warrants	-	-	-
Redeemable Preferred Stock	-	-	-
Preferred Stock	-	-	-
Common Stock	417,000	423,000	431,000
Retained Earnings	49,105,000	43,854,000	40,206,000
Treasury Stock	-	-	-
Capital Surplus	2,596,000	2,425,000	2,135,000
Other Stockholder Equity	1,053,000	2,694,000	851,000
Total Stockholder Equity	**53,171,000**	**49,396,000**	**43,623,000**
Net Tangible Assets	**$40,983,000**	**$38,593,000**	**$33,741,000**

Income Statements

As equally important as the balance sheet is the income statement. The income statement has two very simple, yet important sections: Revenues & Expenses. The revenue section shows all income that the company had come in during the period and the cost of that revenue (also known as cost of goods sold). The difference between the two is the gross profit or margin. The higher the margin generally the better.

The expense section on the other hand has all expenses that the company incurred during the period such as rent, payroll, research fees, and all others items grouped in sections that cost the company money during the period.

The difference from the income section and the expense section is the net profit (or loss). The larger the profit, generally the better for stock prices and when push comes to shove is the real reason a company's stock price either appreciates or declines. The numbers derived from the income statement are the numbers used to calculate the company's earnings per share (EPS) and price to earnings ratio (P/E).

So it is important to educate yourself in these areas and become a seasoned investor instead of someone who takes advice from a financial advisor, who probably doesn't even have investments of his own, and if he does, they're probably not the same investments he's been pressured to sell you.

Below is a copy of a recent Wal-Mart income statement as copied from the Yahoo! Finance page.

View: **Annual Data**	Quarterly Data	All Numbers Are In Thousands		
Period Ending	**31-Jan-06**	**31-Jan-05**	**31-Jan-04**
Total Revenue	315,654,000	287,989,000	258,681,000
Cost of Revenue	240,391,000	219,793,000	198,747,000
Gross Profit	**75,263,000**	**68,196,000**	**59,934,000**
Operating Expenses			
Research Development	-	-	-
Selling General and Administrative	56,733,000	51,105,000	44,909,000
Non Recurring	-	-	-
Others			
Total Operating Expenses			
Operating Income or Loss	**18,530,000**	**17,091,000**	**15,025,000**
Income from Continuing Operations			
Total Other Income/Expenses Net	248,000	201,000	164,000
Earnings Before Interest And Taxes	18,778,000	17,292,000	15,189,000
Interest Expense	1,420,000	1,187,000	996,000
Income Before Tax	17,358,000	16,105,000	14,193,000
Income Tax Expense	5,803,000	5,589,000	5,118,000
Minority Interest	(324,000)	(249,000)	(214,000)
Net Income From Continuing Ops	11,231,000	10,267,000	8,861,000
Non-recurring Events			
Discontinued Operations	-	-	193,000
Extraordinary Items	-	-	-
Effect Of Accounting Changes	-	-	-
Other Items	-	-	-
Net Income	**11,231,000**	**10,267,000**	**9,054,000**
Preferred Stock And Other Adjustments	-	-	-
Net Income Applicable To Common Shares	**$11,231,000**	**$10,267,000**	**$9,054,000**

Types of Income

It's important to know that there are three different types of income and that they all get treated differently for tax purposes. It sounds crazy, but the income that requires sweat and blood is taxed heavier than income that is received without lifting a finger. It sounds backwards, but instead of fighting with it, I recommend adjusting your game plan so the laws become in your favor. The three different types of income are earned income, passive income, and portfolio income.

Earned Income

Earned income is the most commonly received income. When working on a job, the income that is received is considered earned income as it was worked for, thus earned. Earned income is taxed at the highest rates possible and can be as high at 35 percent.

Passive Income

Passive income is income that is received without any or much work being done by the investor. Income from having an ownership interest in a limited partnership would be considered passive income, as well as income received from real estate. Passive income is taxed the same way as earned income, except that most real estate income will be tax free due to the multiple tax deductions involved in having investment real estate.

I would much rather prefer passive income versus earned income, as it symbolizes that I am receiving income without lifting a finger. As with earned income, a person can only get it from one place at a time as they can only be in one place at a time. With passive income, because it generally doesn't require the investors' presence, it can be received form multiple places at once.

Portfolio Income

Portfolio income is income that is received from having ownership in paper assets such as stocks, bonds, and mutual funds. Dividends from stocks and interest from bonds are examples of portfolio income. Portfolio income is generally taxed at much lower rates than earned and passive income, thus making it more attractive, as this is another form of income that doesn't need to be worked for.

Capital Gains & Losses

Assets such as stocks and bonds are considered capital assets. If a capital asset is sold for more than it was paid for, it is recognized as a capital gain. On the other hand, if a capital asset is sold for less than it was paid for, then it is considered a capital loss. If the capital asset is held for a minimum of one year before it was sold at a profit, then it would be considered a long-term gain.

The good thing about long term capital gains is that they are taxed at a maximum rate of 15 percent versus 35 percent like short-term capital gains. Dividends paid on stocks held for a minimum of 60 days are also taxed at a maximum of 15 percent.

Summary of Chapter

The accounting basics that were discussed in this chapter are only a small fraction of accounting concepts, but are the important basics needed to invest wisely in your mission to becoming financially free.

From reading and carefully analyzing a company's income statement, to making investment decisions with the tax rate of different forms of income in mind, this chapter is very important and needs to be understood very well if someone is going to consider becoming an active investor. Without the knowledge that was presented in this chapter, a person will make unintelligent investment decisions, when the option of making an informed decision was just a few steps away. For more accounting information, visit the world popular www.BlackBusinessSmart.blogspot.com.

CHAPTER 11
WHAT YOU NEED TO KNOW ABOUT CONTRACTS

According to "West Business Law" a contract is "a promise or set of promises for the breach of which the law gives a remedy, or the performance of which the law in some way recognizes as a duty." In simple terms, a contract is an agreement that can be enforced in court.

A contract is formed when an offer is made by one party and accepted by another party. This is considered the agreement. For example, if I offered to cut someone's grass for $50 and that person accepted my offer, then we have an agreement, which in essence is considered a contract.

Elements of a Contract

In order to fully understand how forming a contract works, it is important to understand the elements that make up a contract. There are four elements that must be in place to have a legal contract. If one of the elements is missing or goes unfulfilled than the contract is void, thus not a contract enforceable in court.

Agreement

The first element that must be present to have a legal contract is an agreement. As stated previously an agreement is formed when there is an offer as well as an acceptance. One party must offer something, and another party must accept what was offered.

Consideration

The second element of legal contract is consideration. Consideration means that there must be something of value being offered or exchanged. If there is no consideration involved, then there is not a legal contract in the eyes of the court.

For example, if I entered into a contract with my mom to keep my television on BET, and there was nothing of value involved or being exchanged, even if this agreement was in writing, it would not be considered a legal contract as there is no consideration or anything of value involved.

Contractual Capacity

The third element of a contract that must be present is contractual capacity. Contractual capacity means that all parties involved must have the ability to legally be obligated in a contract. This means that all parties must be mentally competent, and have the means to negotiate for themselves a fair and reasonable agreement.

For example, if I went into a contract with a person with mental retardation that doesn't have the ability to represent themselves properly to look out for their best interest, then this would not legally be considered a contract if it was provable that one of the parties did not have contractual capacity.

In addition to being mentally competent, all parties must have the legal ability to enter into the contract being agreed upon. For example, if I had no relation with General Motors, but I negotiated on their behalf to sell 1,000 brand new Cadillac trucks for $20,0000 a piece, then this would not be a legal contract, as I didn't have contractual capacity to enter into a contract on the behalf of General Motors.

Legality

The fourth and final element that must be present to have a legal contract is legality. Legality means that the contract's purpose must be to carry out an act or duty that is legal and not against the law.

For example, if I went into a contract as a pimp with a prostitute that would secure her as a sex employee of mine for three years, this would not be a legal contract as the act of prostitution that is to be carried out is illegal.

Another example would be if I entered into a contract with a drug dealer to buy a large amount of cocaine for a specific price. Because the act that is to be carried out is illegal, this would not constitute a legal contract that could be enforced in court.

Written vs. Oral Contracts

In the majority of cases, a contract can be created orally or in writing. Although the court has enforced several contracts that were created orally, I don't recommend forming oral contracts, as it becomes one party's word versus the other if there is ever a dispute. Generally when a contract isn't in writing, it becomes very hard to prove, especially if one of the parties has a sudden case of memory loss and doesn't admit to the agreement.

This is often the case when there is an oral agreement and one of the parties no longer wants to be committed to the agreement. It's very unethical, but it's something that is generally gotten away with in the majority of cases, unless the plaintiff can somehow prove the oral agreement existed with tape recordings or credible witnesses.

To give you an illustration of how this could pan out, I'll give you the story of Heidi and her next door neighbor Mark. The day after Thanksgiving, Heidi went to Wal-Mart early in the morning to catch a great sale on a new television set. It was a nice upgrade from the television that she already had.

Her neighbor Mark, only had a black and white television, and when he saw her bringing the new television in, he asked if she was interested in selling her old television. After some mild negotiations they agreed on a price of $100. Mark said he would give her the money after 10:00 when the bank opened.

At about 8:00 that morning, there was a change in plans on behalf of Mark. A friend of his called him and told him about the after Thanksgiving Day sale that was going on at Wal-Mart. This gave Mark the idea that he could buy a new television for that same $100 that he was going to pay Heidi for her television.

Mark of course went to Wal-Mart, and purchased a new television at a great price. When he pulled up in front of the house, Heidi was looking out of the window as 10:00 was approaching and thought that Mark was coming back with the $100 to buy her television. However, she was surprised when she saw Mark take a television out of his backseat.

After he took the television in the house, Heidi confronted him and he told her that he didn't want to buy her television anymore. Heidi complained about them having an agreement, which was to no concern of Mark.

Heidi lived by certain strict principles and didn't like to be disrespected so she shot him....Okay it didn't go that far, but she did take him to small claims court. While in court, Mark lied and told the judge that he only said that he might be interested in buying her television and that Heidi must have heard him wrong. Since there were no witnesses available, the judge had to dismiss the case as there was no proof of the contract. It was just his word versus hers.

On the other hand, if Heidi would've had this agreement in writing signed by Mark, the court would've been able to enforce the agreement and force Mark to either buy the television for the agreed upon $100, which is considered "specific performance" or give Heidi "damages" (cash reward for wrongdoing) of the $100 that she was supposed to receive for the sale of her television.

The above story should give you a good clarification on my opinion and feelings on oral contracts. If the person you are dealing with has the ability to lie or be unethical at times (every human being), than a written contract is always the way to go.

Statute of Frauds

Although many contracts can be formed both orally and in writing, there are certain contracts that must be in writing in order to be enforceable. The law that governs this is the "Act for the Prevention of Frauds and Perjuries of 1677. This is commonly referred to as the Statute of Frauds, and states that certain contracts can only be enforced with a signed agreement.

There are five types of contracts that fall under the Statute of Frauds as they are listed below:

Contracts Involving Interest In Land

An agreement to sale land and all other real property (anything attached to the land) is only considered an enforceable contract if it's in writing and signed by all parties. This means that if someone agrees orally to buy a home from someone at a certain price, and then changes their mind, it is totally legal to do so, as there was never a legal contract in place since it was not in writing.

I find it very important to have this type of contract only enforceable in writing, as someone with an unethical witness could lie and say that there was an agreement with a third party to sell a house for a very low price. Without the Statute of Frauds in place, a judge might find this believable and order "specific performance", which would force the owner of the home to sell it at the specified price made up by the unethical plaintiff.

The One Year Rule

The One Year Rule refers to contracts that by their terms cannot be carried out within a year from the date of creation. Any agreement that cannot be carried out within a years time must be in writing to be enforceable. For example, if I agreed to buy my best friend's car for $200 in a year from now, this agreement could only be enforceable in court if it is in writing and signed by both parties.

This is very important, as many oral contacts go bad due to memory loss or what is appeared to be a case of memory loss. A lot of things can happen in the time span of one year, and it is very good that all contracts that cannot be carried out for a minimum of one full year must be in writing to be enforceable.

Collateral Promises

A collateral promise is one where a third party assumes the debt or obligations of a primary party to a contract. For example, if my mother borrowed $10,000 from the bank, I could agree to pay the money back as a collateral promise if she doesn't make payment when it is due. This would have to be in writing to be enforceable. If in writing and my mother didn't make payment when due, I would be held liable for making payment.

Promises Made In Consideration of Marriage

A promise made in consideration of marriage must be in writing to be enforceable in court. For example, If my wife's dad offered to pay me $10 million to marry his daughter (I'm not cheap!) and I accept, this agreement would have to be in writing to be enforceable in court.

Another example would be if my wife offered to buy me a car if I married her. After we got married, this would only be enforceable in court if it was agreed upon in writing. If this wasn't agreed upon in writing, even if she admits to promising it, it would not be enforceable in court, as this type of agreement can only be formed in writing and must be signed by all parties.

Contracts For The Sale of Goods Priced At $500 or Greater

The fifth and final type of contract that must be in writing to be enforceable is when it involves the sale of goods priced at $500 or more. For example, if Heidi had agreed to sale her television set to mark for $500, than there would have been no cause to go to court, as an oral agreement to sale a good for over $500 must be in writing to be considered a legal contract.

Another example of this would be if I was at a car lot and agreed orally to buy a car at a certain specified price. If while walking back inside the car dealership I happen to change my mind, there would be no legal ramifications to prevent me from doing so. Also, if the car salesman went back on his word and decided not to sell the car to me for the price we orally agreed on, he could do so without any legal ramifications stopping him from legally doing so also, as any agreement to sale goods priced at over $500 must be in writing to do so.

Ambiguous Terms

Sometimes contracts are written and may contain ambiguous or unclear language. This is sometimes done on purpose by unethical individuals to perform trickery, and sometimes it is done by mistake as many words and phrases have more than one meaning. Generally when an ambiguous contract has become a topic of argument in court, the judge will rule the contract's meaning based on what appears to have been the intent of the contract by the language used.

Also, an important note to know, is that when dealing with ambiguous terms in contracts, the court will rule against the party that wrote the ambiguous terms as they are at fault for not using plain and simple English, as is required when drafting contracts.

For example, if I wrote an ambiguous contract that contains material language that has more than one meaning, the court will rule against me and in the other party's favor as I am considered the one at fault for not using clear English. For more information on contracts, visit www.Black-BusinessSmart.blogspot.com.

BUSINESS ARTICLES WRITTEN BY AUTHOR

THE REAL DEAL ON ARTIST ADVANCE MONEY

We've all heard stories of rappers and singers who have never received a royalty check. The first thing we as intelligent human beings think is that the company must be crooked or the artist' team is stealing from them. In some cases both scenarios are possible, but generally, the artist isn't getting any money from record sales because their advance hasn't been recouped

Artist advance money for recording artist is one of the most misunderstood concepts of any business. Unlike various sports such as basketball and football, an artist advance check is not a bonus, but instead is a loan that must be re-paid with artist royalties, and not company profits from the artist' album.

When a recording artist signs a record deal, he or she generally gets an advance of monies from the record company that has the main purpose of financing the production and completion of the artist' album. Depending on the level of the artist, the advance given could be several million dollars, thus creating a longer time frame before the advance is recouped, which is the breaking point for the artist to begin receiving royalties. Other money that must be recouped (depending on the terms of the contract) before an artist receives any royalties includes any money that is spent on video production that is not agreed upon as an expense of the company.

Say for example, a rapper has a lot of buzz in the street. This would obviously force the record label to anticipate a larger amount of records sales than a much less talked about artist. In this case, the rapper has the power to demand a much larger advance, since his buzz is a leverage that has convinced the company that they will make their money back and some with the artist' record sales.

Let's say the company advanced this particular artist $500,000. Although this dollar amount is just a loan, it is fully taxable. After taxes, the artist now has $350,000 to work with. The artist uses $300,000 to fund the production of their CD. This cost included paying producers, engineers, studio fees and songwriters if he or she needed any. The artist has now completed their album and has $50k to spend however they choose. Due to having a good attorney, the artist was able to negotiate the video cost to be fully funded and counted as an expense to the record label. This definitely saved the artist a lot of head ache and avoided any extra unwanted recoupment time before the artist could start receiving royalties.

Now for easy math sake, let's say the artist is set to make $1.50 for every record sold, and the record label receives $10.00 per album sold (or $8.50 after paying the artist his assigned royalty payment of $1.50). Even though the company is receiving $10.00 for every record sold, the advance recoupment is schedule based on the artist royalties and not company profits as stated earlier. Thus in order to re-pay the record label the $500k that the artist owes, he would have to sell 333,333 records, but in all actuality the record label is really receiving slightly over $3.3 million for the sales of 333,333 records ($10 per record x 333,333).

At that point the artist may begin to receive royalties if he is totally recouped and no longer owes the record label any money. This can be very tricky, depending on how the contract was negotiated (if negotiated at all), since other fees may have been charged to the artist and made re-payable to the company such as advertising cost, marketing expenses and many other misc. fees that can add up and make it impossible for the artist to ever break even.

Besides the possibility of giving the artist a little financial stability, advances do generally have a few other benefits, but then again it all depends on if you have the business sense to negotiate a contract, versus just accept anything that the company puts in front of you to sign. An advantage of most advances is that they are generally non-returnable. This means that if the artist never sells enough records to become totally recouped, it is considered the loss of the company, and that is why advances are taxable when received by the artist even though it's just a loan.

Another worthy concept to note is cross collateralization. This is generally only in favor of the record label. Cross collateralization connects any advances or cost assigned to the artist to his future projects. For example, using the above illustration, say the artist only sold 250,000 records versus 333,333 and never was full recouped. He has only recouped $375,000 of the $500,000 that was advanced to him and still owes the company

$125,000. This $125k carries over to the next album (on top of the advance for the next album) that the artist makes for that same record label.

This concept can obviously put the artist into some serious debt with the record label, and can make it so an artist never receives a royalty check especially if the artist never generates enough buzz to receive industry respected record sales.

Overall, artist advance money can be a confusing topic, but not if an artist takes the time to go out and read about the business and educate themselves on the basics as well as advanced concepts. To anyone interested in learning the real music *business*, I recommend reading "All You Need to Know About the Music Business" by Donald S. Passman.

How To Increase Your Economic Worth

With One Asset After Another

Every so often, I hear people describe how much money they are worth based on how much they make with their current employer, or by how much money is in their bank account or 401k. Although these numbers can have an impact on how much you're worth, they are by no means the determining factor.

A persons' worth is determined by adding the value of all their assets and then subtracting whatever liabilities they have. According to GAAP, (generally accepted accounting principles) which is followed by most accountants, assets are anything that you own that have some market value to it, and liabilities are debts you owe, and may be tied to an asset. For example, according to GAAP your home is considered an asset and the mortgage note is considered a liability. The difference between the two is considered equity (i.e. House worth $150k- House debt $123k= equity of $27k).

Building your net worth can be accomplished in a number of different ways, but the two most common are buying appreciating/income producing assets and by paying down all your debts. With paying down your debts, it is important to start with the liability that has the highest interest rate. For example, if you have 3 maxed out credit cards with interest rates of 9%, 14%, and more commonly 29%, make it a priority to pay of the credit card with the 29% rate first, while just making the minimum payments on the other two. Then use this same process for all your liabilities.

Creating and building assets is the fun part. You should make it a habit to use some of your hard earned money each month to purchase an appreciating or income producing asset. Even if it's only $50 a month, it's better than nothing.

Personally, my favorite assets appreciate in value, and are the ones that I can borrow the money to buy, with someone else paying back the note each month. Yeah you guessed it. Real Estate is my asset of choice, and I'll tell you why.

In December of 2004 I purchased a duplex up north, with a monthly PITI (principle, interest, taxes, & insurance) expense of $750. When I bought it, the lower level was already being rented out for $450, so I lived upstairs. I had to live in it for at least a couple of months because I promised the lenders that I would *owner occupy* it, which gave me better financing options. After six months I moved out and hired a property mgmt company to rent out the upstairs and maintain the property. Now the property collects $850 in rent and only has an expense of about $800 a month including the property mgmt fees.

Even though I purchased the home with no money down, and don't pay anything for it monthly out of my pocket, I get to enjoy the tax benefits of home ownership, and enjoy all the equity the home builds. So if in 10 years the home is worth $50k more than I paid for it, and I sell it for market value, I as the owner of the home receive all the proceeds from appreciation, without having to share any of the gains with the bank who borrowed me the money or the nice tenants who paid my mortgages for me all those years. And this is why real estate is my asset of choice.

LIFESTYLE HABITS OF THE RICH THAT STAY RICH

Take Care of Business & Business Will Take Care Of You

We've all heard the stories before. One celebrity after another who went from living on top of the world, to filing bankruptcy and being forced to sell their home, cars and sometimes even their spouse's wedding rings to make ends meet. It's a terrible story, but the fact is that most people's biggest financial troubles start when they see their first million or so.

The problem is that most people who loose their fortunes don't make plans on how they're going to keep their income far surpassing their expenses. And before they know it, they're in a hole they can't get out of. Many people think that once they're rich they can just spend as much money as they want to, no matter how much money they have coming in every month.

The difference between people who fall off and loose their fortunes and people like Bill Gates, Warren Buffet and Arthur Blanks is that they all own businesses that provide enough income to allow them to live such extravagant lifestyles and continue to grow their net worth at the same time. Therefore, it's not really them that pay for their lifestyles but their businesses, in the sense that they may not have to work hard at all, but have a system in place that provides them with hundreds of millions or billions annually in income.

What people like Gates, Buffet, and Blanks do is exemplifying living off your assets. What they do is use their initial fortunes to buy or build lifelong cash producing assets such as football teams, and Fortune 500 companies. This approach is totally opposite of what most people do who fall off from their fortunes, that get their money and right away buy a depreciating Mercedes, depreciating jewelry, and anything else they can get their hands on that depreciates in value as soon as they touch it.

I'm not saying you can't have these nice things, because you can. Just don't pay for them with your money, but instead put your money to work for you, and then let your asset that produces continual income pay for all the nice things you want. Let's say you want that new CLS 500 Benz. Instead of going out to buy one with your own money, buy a small apartment building that has enough excess income monthly to pay for the note. For example, let's say you find a luxury car with a hefty price tag of $60,000. With a 4 year note and a low A.P.R. we may be looking at a monthly payment of approximately $1,500.

To overcome this large payment without it handicapping your financial situation, I recommend finding an investment property that can pay for this note, while appreciating in value at the same time. In this situation I would get in contact with a commercial lender that originates mortgages on small to mid size commercial properties. After being approved for a commercial loan I would hire a realtor (since their pay comes from sellers' funds only) to help me find a profitable property that has at least $1,500 in net income monthly.

Following this method would give you a new Mercedes that you don't have to pay for, as well as an asset that will grow in value and continue to give you income long after the car has been paid off. That way, you're not paying for the depreciating toy, but instead your asset is, and that is what it means to live off your assets.

In addition to real estate, most financially fit people also invest in the stock market by way of individual stocks & mutual funds. Over the last 75 years the stock market has grown on average of 10% annually. Assuming you have $1 million invested in the stock market, using the average growth rate of 10%, the investor would gain $100,000 a year by putting their money to work for them.

Before investing in the stock market, I do recommend any potential investor to educate themselves on the market and economy as a whole. There are a lot of tricks and traps (ways to loose your money) involved in the stock market, so one must be prepared mentally & emotionally for all possibilities. For detailed knowledge on the stock market I do recommend reading "The Rules For Growing Rich" by David A. Lereah. Once you're ready to begin your investment career, I suggest researching reputable companies and finding a financial advisor (aka traveling salesman) that you feel comfortable with, and one that's willing to be patient and educate you to be in a position to become a successful investor.

Another thing that successful people do is give. Most of them are all big givers, and it is normally not just for a tax write off, because they only get a percentage back of what they gave in tax savings, so throw that myth out the window. They give because they know you reap what you sow. Just like a farmer who plants corn seeds. He plants them because he likes getting more corn once the harvest comes in. So give and it will be given to you.

On a lighter note, one last thing that the wealthy do is play golf. According to Donald Trump, the relaxation of the golf course has helped him come up with some of his best ideas, as well as help him make many business deals with other rich and successful golfers.

If you do these things you'll maintain your fortune and increase your net worth at the same time, and from a financial point of view live happily ever after.

PREPARE FOR RETIREMENT & STILL LIVE GOOD

Living For Today & Tomorrow

As we all know, retirement is one of the last things we think about as young adults. As a matter of fact, it's also one of the last things we think about as mature adults as well. We all know that if we're blessed with the opportunity to live to 70 or 80 years old, that we are going to need a steady income, and it more than likely won't come from full time employment. Nowadays, even if you want to work pass 65, it's hard. Between age discrimination, and medications that call for 16 hours of bed rest, there's not much to do for a livable income after 65 or 70.

To make matters worse, it is often much more expensive to survive during your golden years versus when you were younger. Why? Because it cost more to live. Think

about it. What fees do many older adults have that most 30 year olds don't? More than likely, when you're 30, you don't have nursing home fees, nor a significant amount of prescriptions to keep your vital organs working.

The best way to avoid being poor at 65, is to start saving and investing today. No matter if you're 18 or 35. Start now!!! But how? You might ask. "I can barely pay my bills each month, let alone save." With a re-adjustment that's how. The first thing you can do is prepare a budget each month, and then track where your money *actually* went versus what you budgeted for, and you may be in for a surprise. You didn't realize how that $6 lunch every day at work affected your finances huh? You didn't even budget for it, but some how it cost you over $120 a month.

You find yourself budgeting $75 a month for entertainment (movies, dates, clubs) and realize you spend more than five times ($375) that every month. Sounds bad right? Yeah, I know. Obviously, we all want to have fun and live good, and the good news is we can do all those things and save for retirement at the same time. Let's say we get some discipline and only eat out for lunch once a week. So we save about $100 a month there. That's good. We got something to work with now. Now you might be thinking "I'm going to Visions! (popular Atlanta night club)" And that's fine. Go all you want, but now only spend $310 a month on entertainment instead of the $375 you found yourself spending last month.

Now you got $165 a month to work with, which is about $2,000 a year to invest in a well diversified mutual fund that should earn you about 10% a year on average over 45 years. If you're 25 now, you can invest that $2,000 every year for ten years. You can stop saving at 35 (although I wouldn't recommend it) and let it grow at an estimated 10% every year and at age 65, that $20,000 that you saved up over a ten year period is now worth $611,817. Retirement isn't all that bad now is it? But you must start now, cause if you wait until you're 35 and save $2,000 *every year* until you're 65, it would only amount to about $360,000 at a 10% growth rate. About $250,000 less, even though you invested $40,000 more. Remember if you're young, you got time on your side, so start saving and investing now.

RE-UP!!

How To Use Your 9-5 Money To Finance Your REAL Goals

About 2 years ago, I was given some very important information that I'll always hold on to, and pass down to my children, and if it's God's will, my children's children. The information came from a subordinate, yet supervisor of one of my departments, while I was in management for a fortune 500 company. At the time we were talking about business and some of our entrepreneurial goals when he said "My whole thing is to make sure I'm using them, while they're using me". Speaking about the company we were working for, I knew his statement meant that when I was to leave that I was to make sure I was able to say that I left with something, instead of nothing which is normally the case these days in a 9-5 world.

On many occasions I've heard stories about loyal and faithful employees who gave 10 or 20 years of their life to a company, only to find out that the company is restructuring or better yet downsizing and won't be needing their help anymore. In this case, if the employee wasn't business or investment savvy, they probably left with nothing to show for their long term commitment to the company, while on the other hand the company continues to reap revenues from the thousands of customers that the past employees went out of their way to keep satisfied. This scenario seems very unfair, but in all actuality it is the exact opposite; very fair.

The reason that the above scenario is so fair is because, employees have a choice of where to put their hard earned paychecks. Believe it or not, some employees decide to put all of their discretionary income in Gucci bags and other futile possessions that have no long term chance of an appreciated resale value. While others save up for down payments on their first and second homes, then put a little money each month into a Roth

IRA that grows tax free. Some employees decide to fund their landlords' retirement by paying off their landlords' mortgage for them, while others fund their own retirement, by paying off their own mortgages, and at the same time do themselves a tax favor by deducting the interest paid on the mortgage from their taxable income.

As we all know, life is full of choices that we must make, but the key is to make them with tomorrow in mind, and not just today. Although I do believe that it is important to enjoy the present day, I don't believe it should be done at the expense of having a terrible tomorrow.

To help you understand where I'm coming from, I'll give you the story of Nicole, who very well understood what it meant to use her 9-5 to finance her REAL goals. Nicole was a recent college graduate when she got her first full time job as a paralegal for a prestigious law firm. Her base salary was $37k a year, with the chance of earning a $3k bonus each year if certain goals where met. Now of course she was a hard worker, so she planned to use her $3k bonus at the end of the year to finance her closing cost of her first home.

Now throughout the first year she kept a solid, yet flexible budget, meaning she wasn't tied to it by death, but stayed pretty close to the parameters she set each month. Having this budget in place she was able to see where all of her money was going, and then save $400 each month. Nicole was smart, so she put $200 a month into a savings account to build up her emergency fund for a rainy day or even worse a stormy season, and the other $200 went into her Roth IRA for retirement.

After the first year went by, Nicole had $2,000 in her savings account (she would have had $2400, but she spent $400 on unexpected car repairs), and $2700 in her Roth IRA that had grown in value a little bit, which she couldn't complain about. On top of the money she's already saved this year, she also just got her $3k bonus from her employer that was $2500 after taxes, which was to fund her closing cost on her a new home.

Throughout the year Nicole was focused on buying her first home, so she researched her mortgage companies and found a great mortgage company based in Atlanta, GA. Her loan advisor gave her advice as to how to get her credit in line so she'd be ready by the time her bonus check came.

When she got her check, she pursued an 80/20 mortgage that gave her two separate loans (one for 80% and the other for 20%), but avoided private mortgage insurance that is usually paid by borrowers if they put less than 20% down. Her loan advisor also advised her to write the contract offer with the seller paying 3% of the purchase price in closing cost.

About a month after looking and making various unsuccessful offers, she finally got a purchase agreement on a nice 3 bed, 2 bath, and 2 car garage home about 20 minutes from downtown Atlanta for $130K. Her total *PITI* (principle, interest, taxes and insurance) payment was a little less than $1,000 a month.

With owning her first home, she still wasn't satisfied. She decided to turn her current home into a rental property and buy a new home to live in. About 8 months after buying her first home she had a contract on another home for $140k. When she made the offer on the second home, it was contingent on her securing a contract with a property management company and them securing a satisfactory12 month lease on her current home with quality tenants, which took very little time.

Now Nicole felt a little better about herself. She owned two homes, one of which she didn't have to pay for, since her tenants paid PITI and property management fees, while at the same time having the peace of mind that she was growing equity in both of her homes. Although she felt a little better about herself, she still stayed true to her budget and saving habits. After 5 years, Nicole had $16k in her Roth IRA, $15k in her savings account, and a total of $95K in equity in her two homes and was actually ready to move up and buy another home for $200k, and I'm sure you can imagine how that went.

Nicole was just an example of "How To Use Your 9-5 To Finance Your REAL Goals" that could be done by anyone with a little direction, determination and discipline.

REFERENCE & RECOMMENDED READINGS

1.) *How To Get Started In Real Estate Investing by Robert Irwin, Mc Graw Hill, 2002*

2.) *It Pays To Talk by Carrie & Charles Schwab, Crown Business, 2002*

3.) *Marketing, 6ᵗʰ Edition by Berkowitz, Kerin, Hartley & Rudelius, Irwin Mc Graw Hill, 2000*

4.) *Mortgages 101 by David Reed, Amacom, 2004*

5.) *Own Your Own Corporation by Garrett Sutton, Esq., Warner Business Books, 2001*

6.) *Real Estate Flipping by Mark B. Weiss, Adams Media, 2004*

7.) *Rich Dad Poor Dad by Robert Kiyosaki, Warner Business Books, 1997**

8.) *The Rules For Growing Rich by David A. Lereah, Crown Business, 2000*

9.) *West's Business Law Alternate Edition, by Jentz, Miller & Cross, West, 2002*

---

* is placed by Rich Dad Poor Dad as it is my favorite business book of all time, and laid the grown work to my new financial way of thinking.

ABOUT THE AUTHOR

La'Foy Thomas is a law student at the University of Arkansas, and holds a four year business degree from Upper Iowa University where he graduated with honors. He is a published business/finance magazine writer for several magazines including nationwide Grip Magazine and Miami based Success South Florida Magazine.

La'Foy credits Robert Kiyosaki and Donald Trump for changing his way of thinking financially. First Robert Kiyosaki for laying the solid financial foundation down with "Rich Dad Poor Dad", and secondly "The Art of the Deal" by Donald Trump for teaching him how to think big.

At the age of 20, La'Foy was divinely brought together with his wife Camille, and has been married since April of 2003. La'Foy overcame many obstacles in route to being placed in a position by God to make history. Growing up in the inner city of Milwaukee, WI where pimps and gangsters controlled the streets, La'Foy learned a lot of things that prepared him to write his first novel "No More Pain", which is loosely based on his life story of a black male growing up and out of the ghetto to bigger and better things, very similar to his real life situation. The story is life changing, and is a must read for anyone with aspirations to make it out of a bad situation.

La'Foy is also working on the sequel to "No More Pain" entitled "My Testimony" which is an urban fiction roller coaster ride for the ages. Lastly, La'Foy is also the creator of the world popular Black Business Smart www.BlackBusinessSmart.blogspot.com web blog.

Printed in the United States
65757LVS00008B/103